Potpourri From The Heart

A ROSE OF SHARON COMMUNITY CHURCH
ANTHOLOGY OF LOVE

Copyright © 2014 by Rose of Sharon Community Church. All rights reserved.

Cover Design by Madeline and Jason Evans

Printed in the United States of America

Publishing services by Selah Publishing Group, LLC, Tennessee. The views expressed or implied in this work do not necessarily reflect those of Selah Publishing Group.

The views of the authors' submissions do not necessarily reflect the views of the Rose of Sharon Community Church. They are solely the views of each individual author.

No part of this book may be reproduced, stored in a retrieval system or transmitted in any form or by any means without the prior written permission of the author, except by a reviewer who may quote brief passages in a review to be printed in a newspaper, magazine, or journal.

ISBN: 978-1-58930-293-8
Library of Congress Control Number: 2014907521

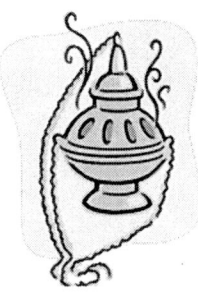

POTPOURRI (po-poo-ree) noun.

Olla Podrida (Spanish) 1. A combination of various incongruous elements.
2. A miscellaneous collection or anthology; a mixture of dried flower petals and spices kept in a jar and used especially to scent the air.

DEDICATION

We Praise and Honor God for giving Sallie Proctor the vision.
To Sallie Proctor for being obedient to the Holy Spirit.
To Bishop Ball for being our life line so that we wouldn't
drift out too far from the peaceful shore!

TABLE OF CONTENTS

Potpourri iii
Dedication iv
Foreword 7
Acknowledgements 9
Special Appreciation 10
Love Note From Bishop 11

1. A Memorial Poem 12
2. Shine 13
3. Free 14
4. God's Love and Mercy 15
5. My Beautiful Daughters 16
6. Wrong 18
7. May 2011 19
8. Manifested Faith 22
9. Shoes 23
10. The Strong Shall Bear the Infirmities of the Weak 24
11. Sisters… There's A Great Campground Awaiting 26
12. A Bountiful Harvest Fulfilled 28
13. You Gave Me Love 30
14. Linen Napkins 32
15. Breast Cancer Survivor 34
16. My Testimony, Praise God! 35
17. Young Girl 36
18. A Blanket of Love 38
19. God Has a Plan 39

20. I Made a Mistake 44
21. Believe God and Have Faith 46
22. Wisdom That Comes From God 48
23. My Story 51
24. Will You Play Catch With Me? 57
25. My Childhood Memories 62
26. Education: Key to a Successful Life 68
27. What Our Youth Need 71
28. I Am Becoming The Woman He Wants Me To Be 74
29. Let It Go 76
30. Toothpaste Squeezing/ Life's Struggles 80
31. Green Beans 84
32. Life Is Not A Gamble 85
33. I Am My Father's Child 90
34. Are We Running On Empty? 94
35. When Nuthin' Is Enough! 99
36. Sweet Multi Pepper Tomato Sauce 102
37. It's Going to Rain (A Family Reunion) 104
38. He Was There All The Time 106
39. Grow Your Own Oprah 113
40. Hard Times Recipe 117
41. Thoughts on Hard Times 118
42. Youth Prayer 123
43. Troubles and Storms 125
44. Sallie's Wise Suggestions 128
45. Untitled - Ode to the child 129

    Contributors 130

Foreword

This book is humbly written. It is a reflection of Love; not fancy or proud. It reflects some of our most vulnerable times. We are in a world that's turned upside down from the way we used to live. You can have all the money in the world one day and lose it the next; you can be happy as a lark right now and by tonight you could be bogged down with grief. You may be in the best of health today and sick with something unchangeable tomorrow. Knowing that life is uncertain yet exciting is food for thought.

The Rose of Sharon Community Church and others from this country as well as other countries, came together to share their stories, poems, recipes and tidbits of life. As you read through this book of love, you will experience life's ups and downs of people who have come through and are still going through some tough times. You will see raw human emotions as well as strength, mercy and grace given to them by God. It is our hope that you will read this book and learn from the things we have learned throughout our lifetimes. There is a little nugget of knowledge in every entry from the youngest to the eldest writer.

This book is an answer to many prayers. We wanted God to show us how to talk to people who are hurting in many different ways. Some crying loudly, others in silence. Through the leading of the Holy Spirit, God has allowed us to minister to you with non-judgmental hearts and a burden for lost souls. We wanted to let you know that many of us have made it through some difficult circumstances. Make no mistake; we are all in this together. We are told to "Love our neighbors as we love ourselves" and this publication is our way of showing that love. Our church motto is **"I am only one, but I am one. I cannot do everything, but I can do something. What I can do, I ought to do. What I ought to do, by the Grace of God I will do."**

For such a time as this... God Bless you all and I pray that this won't be the last time you hear from us.

Love, Sallie

ACKNOWLEDGEMENT

Our deepest thanks to Bishop M. LaVerne Lattimore Ball for her love of people, her kindness and compassion towards others and especially her unwavering faith in our Lord and Savior Jesus the Christ. She has been with us on this journey from the very beginning. Bishop's love and prayers inspired us and encouraged us to keep going when times and people were hard and we felt tired and broken. Her presence was felt every step of the way. We thank God for our Bishop and for the strength that He gave to her to carry the weight of this project.

> *"Hold fast the form of sound words, which thou hast heard of me, in faith and love which is in Christ Jesus"*
>
> 2 Tim. 1:13 (KJV)

THE "BOOK TEAM"
GAIL DOWLING
MADELINE EVANS
TRACY FOOSTER
SALLIE PROCTOR

SPECIAL APPRECIATION

Special appreciation given to:

To all who have helped to make this journey challenging and exciting. To God be the glory for all He has done!

A Love Note from the Bishop's Desk:

Beloved,

We honor the Lord for your obedience to the Holy Spirit and for your contribution to this book. Your testimonial as to what God has done in your life may literally save the life of another. Indeed it will surely let someone know that they are not alone, and if God did something for you then He can fix something for them. This book is a combination of all the vital ingredients needed to mend the brokenhearted, to heal the wounded and to encourage those who are lost out there in a cold hard world. People's hearts have been opened up by God to share personal accounts of difficult situations in their lives to show their love of Christ and the blessed hope that we have in Him. Others have shared a lighter side of life to put a smile on your face. Either way my beloved we all have a charge on our lives to tell the story. The Bible tells us ***"That is why I am suffering as I am. Yet I am not ashamed, because I know whom I have believed, and am convinced that he is able to guard, what I have entrusted to him for that day. (II Tim. 1:12 NIV)***

A special prayer goes to Sallie Proctor, the visionary that God used to bring this publication into fruition. Her commitment, faith, trust and love for God made it easy for her team to catch the vision, work diligently and to give of their time, talent and support to see that the project was completed.

So now, beloved, know that God promises we will never walk alone and that He cares for each and everyone of us. So open your hearts and discover His love and remember: We have a heaven to win, a hell to shun and God to glorify!

ALL MY LOVE,
BISHOP M. LAVERNE LATTIMORE BALL

Not How Did I Die But How Did I Live

In Memory of Eddie "Big Ed" Walls

Not how did I die, but how did I live?
Not what did I gain but what did I give?
The are the units to measure the worth
Of a man as a man regardless of birth.
Not what was my church, not what was my creed?
But had I befriended those really in need?
Was I ever ready with a word of good cheer?
To bring back a smile to banish a tear?
Not what did the sketch in the newspaper say?
But how many were sorry when I passed away?

    With Love,
    Wife Joyce
    Son Peter (Sheila)
    Daughter Debbie
    Grandsons Na'eem, Jihad, Sabir

SHINE

Vulnerabilities damaged my credibility
Killing opportunities, which jammed me
Until I was told to arise and walk into my destiny
Using my authority to step on jealousy and envy
While starving my doubts planting mustard seed trees, split peas
As I cross the seas. Using pain as my ingredient as I spread
my wings into stirring up the gift of poetry flowing through me
by giving you a sample of
My testimony.
Glowing, knowing, victory

—By Mjael Melissa Greene

FREE

When I think about the love of God, it's like being unharmed and untouched. When I think about a happy child, it's like watching the birds fly in the sky. When I think about a child's laughter, it's like feeling the grass withering and the lilies blooming. For these things they toil not, nor do they sow or reap. Are they not better than I? 'Cause being free is what God wants me to be. Receiving comfort when I think about these things.

—By Mjael Melissa Greene

GOD'S LOVE AND MERCY

In October of 1998, I went to R.W.J. Hospital in New Brunswick, NJ to have a test for my heart. After the test, my doctor told me he wanted me to stay there in the hospital.

I had triple bypass heart surgery. I opened my eyes into darkness and saw a globe made of bright, brilliant colors. It looked like cut stones. Never had I seen anything so beautiful. I didn't have a physical body and I had no fear. Afar off was a light with a brighter light shining within. I heard my voice saying, "Who can go there?" A voice answered, saying "All who want to". "Let me get a closer look", I said. I woke up in the recovery room.

During my recovery at home, I went to my doctor for a check-up. He told me if I had gone home on the day of the test, I would never have made it back to the hospital for surgery. I would have had a massive heart attack.

—JAF

MY BEAUTIFUL DAUGHTERS

Independent though you may think, yet you may never be complete; without having a meaningful relationship with me.

Daughters I can show you how beautiful I made you. From me you came; so come back to me and I will show you the dreams I dreamt for you and the beauty I placed within. That which never can be reached without having a meaningful relationship with me.

First I must cleanse the enemy from within, and the hurt from the pain that you carry from people and men, who used you. Now the emptiness that confused you, while searching for a love that could never truly love you, only because you never looked toward the one who created you.

I will satisfy your every need spiritually and teach you how to be who I created you to be. I won't confuse you or mistreat you in any way. I surely won't play those silly games trying to mislead you but I will challenge you to respect yourself as a daughter of mine.

If you decide to reconnect with me instead of connecting with men who can only show you their physical love because they are too disconnected from me. I will show you why I called you. I will rise up a prince for my princess. If you choose to reconnect with me then there will be nor more foolishness. As you begin to set your eyes on me, watch all the dreams I showed you come true because you chose a relationship with me.

Many daughters have done virtuously, but thou excellest them all. Favour is deceitful, and beauty is vain: but a woman that feareth the Lord, she shall be praised. –Prov. 31:29-30

—Jeffrey G. Mitchell, Sr.

WRONG

My relationship with Christ is not that strong
I need to change that
I know it's wrong
At night I would lay
And contemplate my day and
I would have to will myself to pray
Talking to my Lord is what needs to be done
It shouldn't be hard
But sincere and even fun
I'm still young, not even twenty
But I've always come to church
Though not plenty
Rose of Sharon is my home
Yet instead of the sanctuary
It's the streets I roam
I'm not really sure of my relationship with God
The lukewarm stage is what I've been told I am in
Yet every time I do wrong
I'm asking Him to forgive my sins
I know He has unconditional love for me
The light is what I'm striving to see
I'm trying my hardest no to stray
I pray to Him pleading to help me find the way
Because I know the devil is a liar
And Jesus is my rock my soul my fire

—Keyshawna Johnson

May 2011

"If this doesn't work, it will have to be removed". Those were the words spoken by my doctor in October 2009 after a procedure he had performed in April had failed. He was referring to my ever-ailing esophagus and the fact that it just wasn't working as it should.

My problem developed in my late teens and the next 20 years of on going procedures will have had taken its toll on me. Procedures like stretching with long rubber tubes inserted in the throat; balloon dilatations to expand the esophagus, Botox–to freeze my stomach muscles and other surgical procedures that came along with the possible threat of Cancer.

I was told that my esophagus would have to be taken out. The purpose of one's esophagus is to move food (after swallowing) from the throat to the stomach in order to begin the digestion process. When that passageway and the muscles surrounding it become sluggish or stop working properly, food gets "stuck" but then eventually trickles through from physical movement and gravity.

I prayed and prayed and prayed that one day this would pass from me. Many times I had asked God," Why me?" and received the answer "Why not me?" I thought on David's words to God in Psalm 139 declaring how he knew that God knew about him before he was conceived and knows everyday thereafter. It made me realize that come what may, God is the author and finisher of my faith. However, having the problem worsen over time I realized that I had taken my family through enough scares, emergency room visits and testing and needed to make a permanent fix. That didn't mean that I didn't have fear about the procedure and what was so frightening was that I hadn't ever known or heard of anyone who had this same problem. I even had a hard time finding a surgeon with a proven track record who could perform such a risky operation. Little did I know then this "problem" that I had endured for twenty years had been the easy part.

In January 2010 I decided to go through with the surgery. I had exhausted all my research from the library, bookstores, various doctors and on the Internet. Strangely enough, sometimes too much research will leave you more frightened than not knowing at all. (Don't trust everything you read on the Internet!) In June of 2010 I prepared myself by taking a leave of absence from work. I had the surgery on the 13th and thought I would be home a few days later. Not so. Although the actual removal of my esophagus was a success, the rest of my body was not ready for the after shock and quickly let me know. My hospital stay was approximately five weeks. It included two different hospitals in two different states, blood transfusions, x-rays, the drainage of fluid from my lungs, breathing difficulties, an abdominal feeding tube, countless medications and on going doctor's visits. Recovery was long and intense and there were many days that I didn't think that I would survive, but thanks be to God, I did.

To anyone reading this testimony, know that we all must go through the things in life and the ONLY way to get through them successfully is with God. If you are blessed enough to live to a certain age, at some point you will more than likely go through medical issues, financial pressures, job strains, broken relationships, the loss of close family members and friends and other trials and tribulations just to name a few. Know that the Bible tells us that God will never leave us nor forsake us (Heb. 13:5) and we can make it if we just trust Him.

The outcome, I am happy to say is that I am healed of all the side effects from the surgery. Each time I look in the mirror, I see my "battle scar" staring back at me in the form of a three inch scar on the left side of my neck where my stomach was moved up through my chest and abdomen and replaced the area where my esophagus was removed. Medical Science is great but God is amazing! I give Him thanks and praise for bringing me through the process. I also praise Him for placing people in my life like my husband, my daughter, extended family and friends and church members who helped me make it through. I pray that I am able to encourage someone with my testimony to go forward and trust Him to direct your path. Seek His will in all you do and He will show you which path to take (Prov. 3:6 NLV).

—Lynell Billingsley-Downer

MANIFESTED FAITH

I will hold on
I will hold on until the day of reckoning
I will keep the faith
I will keep the faith until the day that I no longer need faith
Faith will be manifested on the day
The day that I too will stand at the gates
Oh the glory
Oh the joy
What magnificence
The joy of seeing His face
And once and forever to feel Your sweet embrace
So I must hold on
Until my faith is manifested
When we see our Father's face

—Evang. Adrianne Smiling

SHOES

This is a story about shoes and how they impact our lives.

One Sunday morning, two parishioners were in need of Special Prayer so at the end of service they both went up to the Altar. They hadn't known each other very well but from time to time they would speak to one another in passing. While standing in the aisle waiting to kneel in prayer, one parishioner turned to the other gave her a big hug and told her that Jesus loved her and so did she. Now the first parishioner knew that the second parishioner was going through a terminal illness and was prompted by the Holy Spirit to give her words of comfort. The other parishioner thanked her and turned to walk away; when the first one said to her "And girl you are wearing those shoes!" You see, they both had a passion for shoes, so one Sunday morning a relationship was formed because of a pair of shoes and their need for special prayer.

We never know by what means or channels the Lord will use us. This time it was through a pair of shoes. Shoes have a way of bringing people together. Sometimes shoes even bring us to the Lord.

This story is in memory of **Michelle Allen** my sister in Christ who had a passion for shoes and was lead to another Christian, Delois Langford with the same passion for shoes. **Walk on Michelle, now you can walk all over God's Heaven!**

THE STRONG SHALL BEAR THE INFIRMITIES OF THE WEAK

It was 58 degrees outside in the night
A March night which could have been 30 degrees
As I rounded Joyce Kilmer
Making a right onto New Street
Their presence filled my senses
The young, the old, the little girl with
The pink quilted jacket trimmed in white fur
Sitting silently next to her dad
Some had blankets
Some without, sitting on white resin chairs
Folding aluminum chairs
Some stood rocking back and forth to
Stave off the boredom of waiting
Where do they bathe after a full night of
Wishing the night would be over
Waiting in line for 50 slots for a home on
Section 8
It is a hope, a desperate chance
If they are not lucky to be
A chosen lottery winner
They place their names on a list and wait
And wait and wait for another 24 months
This line screams of the uncertainty of life
Lives hang precariously above the chasm

Potpourri From The Heart

One side shouting wants
One side softening the impending fall
For those who cannot "make it" among the blessed
How much is needed for solvency
All possess a job that can actually take care of our needs
Housing, food, clothing
It is a question without a tangible answer
We are on the verge of a bankrupt, vacuous existence
The inequitable distribution of fish to feed us
The absence of knowledge of how to repeat
This action for the masses, un-earth the
Echoed verse within His text
That the strong shall bear the
Infirmities of the weak

—Beverly Y. Murdock

SISTERS... THERE'S A GREAT CAMPGROUND AWAITING

Yes, Jesus is the answer
We need His loving care
Just rest with quiet patience
Seeking Him in daily prayer
Place yourself completely
In God's loving arms
No worries, no doubts, no fears
To cause you any harm
He's made a way out of no way
Opened doors we thought were closed
God's dream for us is still intact
His love just flows and grows
Even when others forsake you
Or do you any wrong
Say a prayer, shake it off
Be strong and then move on
The Master is our foundation
Let nothing turn you around
Your faith shall not be quenched
For you stand on solid ground
Too many storms a-raging
Too heavy is the night
Take God's yoke upon thee
To make those burdens light

There is a fountain filled with blood
Flowing from Emanuel's veins
Praise God to wash away our sins
And all our guilty stains
Be grateful for all struggles
Let joy ring in your soul
We've come a mighty long way
Not to be sheltered from the cold
God's promise is still standing
To take good care of you
Known as the greatest physician
There's nothing He can't do
No time for weariness sisters
There's a strong Man in our home
His name is King Jesus
Won't forsake you or leave you alone
Sisters… There's a great Campground a-waiting
So lift others as you climb
Anchor until the victory is won
Leave not one sister behind

—Sandra H. Murphy

A BOUNTIFUL HARVEST FULFILLED

Dedicated to the Visionaries, Administration, Board of Trustees, Physicians, Staff, Volunteers & Friends of the Women's Health and Counseling Center

She was the visionary, from the beginning.
Centered in the neighborhood, founding the "Clinic"
An open door in her home to offer care for the countless ones
Falling through the cracks unable to afford treatment
With little or NO insurance…
SHE said yes above the hum of a sanctimonious few who
Raised their pious noses in the air
As she dared to care for "those" people.

From this small beginning the numbers grew from hundreds to
Thousands and they have become whole
They respond to early detection and are **SAVED!**
Those outside its Borough borders seek her refuge.
They are soothed with the Balm of Gilead.
They take the route of responsibility for their medical health.
Seeking solutions in the midst of an insurance card society
Where money talks a <u>little</u>
And the lack of it speaks to the closed doors of care.

This place has become a haven warming hearts along the way.
They apply color to the welcome mats and **INSTANTLY**
Their blood pressure lowers because they are comforted.
They can hear the bilingual rhythm of communication
And they know they will be understood.

It has grown from the faith of a mustard seed,
An idea in the mind of one who **DARED** to think outside
The walls of conformity to rescue those who need care most.
She begot HIM and HE begot Them and They became We…
Filling the souls, curing the disease, calming the fears, erasing the pain,
Answering the question why and responding with "no fee for today".

They laugh, they cry and they receive that which they **NEED!**
Their prescriptions and filled, they return to work, they bear healthy
Children, they remain productive members of society
And they can erase one of many worries from their slate
And the "dream of a Bountiful Harvest is fulfilled!

—Dr. Beverly Y. Murdock

YOU GAVE ME LOVE

He started as a dream, a hope in the womb.
He is the image of Father nurtured by Mother.
He loved Father.
He loved father called to glory. Called to glory too soon.
He loves Father.

You nourished his soul.
You made him whole. You filled his heart.
You shared your grief and made him strong.
You nourished his soul.

He drank your love. Filled his heart, nourished his soul.
He watched you grow. Hallelujah! Thank you Lord.
He was a boy, then man. Proud and tall does he stand.

I have what you left.
I share with you your greatest gift.
The fruit of your love,
The joy of your kiss.
I know what is inside of you.
Strong Mother, loving Mother,
And remember Father.

Love
Love sure grew.
Love was nurtured with what you knew.
God always knew
Sent him to me nourished by you.

You gave me the man.
The man I go to. Go through.
Man nourished by woman.
Woman loved by man.
Nourishing the soul of the man as only a son's mother can.
Until he is Man.

Thank you Mother
YOU GAVE ALL and then…
YOU GAVE ME LOVE

Presented to Mrs. Ardell Smiling in honor of her love, wisdom and guidance to our family with Jesus forever as the head of her life.

—By Adrianne Smiling

LINEN NAPKINS

In Memory of Great-grandmother Ina Hoffman Rigby

Linen Napkins sit with graceful appointment
Upon her table in just the right position
Never too far to the left

Not a wrinkle was noted on the
Crisp linen tablecloth
Each corner eyeing its counterpart
Matching point for point

The water glass was filled
One-quarter inch from the top
Not an eighth or one sixteenth
The dinner plates sat between each table setting
Glistening, Ivory fresh, banded in delicate blue roses

All teacups sat upon their saucers
Attentive to their task, ever watchful
For the appointed hour
When they step upon the stage
Enclosing the heavenly scented brew
From Columbia

Serving dishes lay in wait to be
Heavily laden with turkey, duck, ham and such

Fine wicker baskets lined
With coordinated napkins await the
Hot buttered rolls kneaded, rolled and baked
Early in the morning

Her hands orchestrate a fine food symphony
Planned weeks in advanced
Scrutinized by the palates of the great grands and grands
Fathers and sons

Thankful daughters were blessed with just one day of rest
Knowing that the day would end all too soon
And they would take center stage

—Beverly Y. Murdock

BREAST CANCER SURVIVOR

I am a Christian. I'm saved and living right. I love the saints, give abundantly and play by the rules. I am a loyal friend, a good citizen and model church member. I had mammograms annually but none of that mattered. I got cancer.

After my annual mammogram of 2001, the technician called the Chief of Radiology for a consultation of the results. There was a visible lump in my breast and the radiologist suggest that is should be removed as soon as possible. He exclaimed how did this happen and advance so far? I thought "oh yeah, cancer's not bad enough, now I need a mastectomy."

I began my road to wellness with God, hope, and faith. I was blessed to continue my daily schedule. I went to church on Sunday morning. Presided over a meeting on Monday evening. I had surgery on Tuesday morning. Wednesday I went home (drainage attached) and by Friday I was out being honored at The Westwood dining hall in Garwood, NJ as "woman of government" by the Union County Board of Chosen Freeholders.

After surgery I had chemotherapy and radiation for 18 months and I didn't experience any discomfort from the treatment. My favorite Psalm, 121 helped me go through and giving Honor to God I have been cancer free since 2001. If I had ten thousand tongues I couldn't thank Him enough.

MY TESTIMONY – PRAISE GOD

I was healed from diabetes in 1997. The doctor said it couldn't be done and I would have to take medication for the rest of my life. The doctor said "yes" I had it, but the Lord said no I didn't.

When I was diagnosed with diabetes, it was out of control. I knew nothing about the illness. I didn't even know the warning signs. Hosea 4:6 says, "My people are destroyed for lack of knowledge". Knowledge is powerful, Praise God.

In 1997 I threw away my medication because of a bad news report on TV and I stepped out on faith. I began to learn about diabetes, food and technology monitoring machines. I also learned about my glucose level, my A1C% and how to read my lab reports. The bible says "and in all your getting, get understanding". I have understanding now because I learned how to manage diabetes, today I am diabetes FREE. It has been 14 years without medication. God is still in the healing business. We must put faith into action and let it work. We should learn all we can about managing diabetes because knowledge and understanding is powerful. Praise God.

—Dr. Alice Kelly

YOUNG GIRL

Young girl
Never forget how beautiful you are.
You were created by God the bright morning star.
Young girl
Always strive to be your very best.
Even when he tears you down, calls you names
And says that you're never enough.
You keep walking, never look back and stick out you chest.
Young girl
Take your time walking through this life.
Just remember that all things work together for good.
Even the tears, pain and strife.
Young girl
You were chosen to let your light shine.
Just as Mary says,
"I like what I see when I'm walking past the mirror,
because I'm just fine."
Young girl
You don't have to be a victim, a prisoner of your mind,
an after-thought
Let him know that you CANNOT be bought!
You walk in greatness. You're more than just your body.
You define your own destiny and continue to walk in dignity.
Young girl, you're worth it.

I know sometimes you forget that or in most cases, sadly,
you just don't know.
But I'm proud to say that each day you make
more and more progress,
So just continue to grow.
We are all worthy simply because we were born.
Anything worth having is worth the wait.
You've endured some trials; you've been through the fire
And you've weathered the storm.
Young girl
You are a rising star.
Never ever forget how wonderful you are.
Young girl, YOU rock!!!

—Vernae Taylor

A BLANKET OF LOVE

Little voices speak
Before we understand.
All knowing, so soon
Touches gladly accepted
Soothing questioned responses
Inviting warmed, butterfly kisses…
Softened cheeks
Share intimate spaces
With bristled, stubbly beards.
Demonstrated channels of love
Warm tired, weathered hands.
Affirming generations of
Nurtured care.
Listening follows rippled paths
From tiny hearts alive
Willingly challenged by
Tempered, comforting waters.
Filling unfathomed voids.
Connecting dusted particles
In a blanket of love.

—Dr. Beverly Y. Murdock

GOD HAS A PLAN

When Mama died I began to notice that we were poor. I was about ten years old, the youngest of eleven children; there were three of us still at home. I was used to the life of a sharecropper. Most of the black families in Fayette County, Tennessee were sharecroppers as well as some of the Whites in the 1950's. We lived in a small house without indoor plumbing or central heat. I was accustomed to drawing water from the well and using the outhouse. Papa would read the Bible and tell us stories in front of the fireplace or wood stove.

We grew, raised or caught most of our food. Mama's garden had the best mustard, turnip and collard greens, a variety of peas and beans, cabbage, onions, peppers, okra and tomatoes. Papa grew enough watermelons, cantaloupes and corn to sell and feed us. We had chickens for eggs and meat, pigs to eat and cows for milk and butter. We did not eat our cows; they were too valuable. In hard times, Papa could sell one. There were also plums, pears, peaches, apples, blackberries, persimmons and Muscatine grapes on the land. When Papa went to Town, he would buy bananas and comic books for us and flour, sugar and spices for Mama.

Everyday brought something to enjoy. My brother Coleman always had adventures for us and some were risky. Since he was five years older than I was, Mama expected him to look out for me. In exchange for these adventures, if I got hurt I never let

Mama or Papa know. The one time that they found out was when I fell through the ice on a pond after I went out to test it. Even then I did not tell on my brother, but he was in trouble because he took me home nearly drowned and I developed pneumonia. Thank God I recovered. My brother and I continued to explore and take risks for adventure. I credit my brother for contributing to my adventurous spirit. That was one of my character traits that my husband found attractive.

Mama was like the sun. All family life revolved around her nourishing light. She was a magician in the kitchen, able to create a tasty meal from meager supplies. When the ham, bacon and sausage (all raised, prepared and preserved by us) were finished, she made the lightest, tastiest biscuits with her butter, canned preserves and eggs for breakfast. She could even make rabbit, squirrel and possum tasty.

Mealtime was a ritual. One of us would call Papa. Then we would sit at the table and wait for him. When Papa sat down, he said grace then we would each recite a Bible verse. Then Mama would serve Papa's plate and pass the food around the table. Mama always ate last.

From my earliest memory, Mama was sick. She had at least two strokes before she died. I remember hearing that she had died from the last stroke but I did not comprehend the significance of it. I remember my eldest sister Mandy who lived in Chicago, crying under the black walnut tree in the backyard.

Without Mama life was poor. The house seemed dark, smelly, cold and lonely. I began to notice things that I had not noticed before. I was barefoot most of the time. Shoes were to be saved for church and school. Our meals had lost their good flavor and joy. Papa was a loving father, but he was not suited to be both mother and father to three young children. After awhile, I felt lost and wondered if I had a future. Mandy soon took my thirteen-year old sister Roberta to live with her in Chicago.

Then Coleman went to live with Mandy. Coleman was my best friend. When Coleman left, I felt totally abandoned. No more adventures, no more teasing Mr. Sand's mean bull then trying to outrun him before he caught us and no more secretly riding the pigs.

I loved going to school and I always tried to get good grades. I concentrated on school. A couple of years later Papa and my eldest brother Pete decided that I would stay with Pete and his Wife in Memphis and go to school. They thought I was "smart" and Pete and Ethel were willing to give me the opportunity to get a better education. At that time, "colored" students in Fayette County did not have a High School. After eighth grade we attended Fayette county Training School. Papa had only completed sixth grade, Mama completed eighth grade. None of my sisters or brothers achieved a high school diploma although Pete did return to school later in life. The opportunity for me to attend Junior High School in Memphis was God sent.

I praise my brother and sister-in-law for taking me in but I soon discovered that Ethel didn't want me there. I heard them arguing over whether I could stay and I became afraid that I would lose the opportunity to go to school. I knew how to pray because my father was a deacon and my mother was a praying woman. I prayed to be able to stay until I found a place where I was wanted. While I waited, I concentrated on school and tried to be useful and obedient.

When I was ready for high school, Mandy came and took me to live with her and her husband in their apartment on the South side of Chicago. They treated me like I belonged with them and the overcrowded apartment became a real home. Mandy and Mr. Lake worked long hours. There wasn't much supervision, but I had learned discipline at my brother's home and how to do what I needed to do. There were 8-10 people in the six-room apartment. Roberta and I tried to keep the apartment tidy. I got after school and summer jobs to help out. I kept praying. I remember before every difficult exam, I would study. Then before I went to sleep I would pray and put my book under my pillow. When I sat down for my exam, I believed that God would help me.

I will never forget my biology teacher, Mr. Franklin. He encouraged me. He told me that I could go to college. No one in my family had gone to college. No one in my neighborhood had gone to college. The only college graduates that I knew were my teachers. I told Mr. Franklin that I would enlist in the military when I graduated because I knew people who had successful military careers. Mr. Franklin personally took me to the college counselor's office. He told her to make sure that I got a scholarship to college. When Ms. Schneider dragged her feet, Mr. Franklin came back and continued to advocate for me. I graduated from Englewood High School as Salutatorian of my graduating class and attended the University of Illinois on a full academic scholarship. I believe that God sent Mr. Franklin to be His angel for His plan for my life.

In my senior year at university, I became engaged. After we were married we moved to New Jersey. Finally I had a family of my own and a solid middle class lifestyle. I went to Rutgers Law School and when my husband worked in England, I studied at the University of London for a year. I now started practicing law. My husband was successful: our children were excellent students and active in extra curricular activities and sports. My life was full and I thought I had everything I needed. I was comfortable and expecting a smooth life with my husband and two children. We were nominal members of a church. We didn't attend regularly and I had fallen away from my close walk with God. The enemy came to steal and destroy my family. After nearly 25 years of marriage, my husband wanted a divorce. Once again I faced abandonment. I was heartbroken, lonely and afraid. My children, the oldest a college graduate with her own apartment and the youngest who was about to graduate from college were devastated. I prayed and I went back to the Word. I started with Psalms and then I really began to meditate on His Word.

God answered my cry and sent angels. He sent friends. Some that I had neglected over the years gathered around me to hold me up. My daughter would drive more than a half hour to take walks with me. She even joined a gym near me to encourage me, all without our ever discussing the divorce. My son reached out to me and invited me to join him at a conference in Montreal Canada. Two months after the divorce was filed, I met a good strong man who was confident enough to comfort me when I cried for the family I had lost. He was also a man who revived in me the spirit of adventure that I had shared with my brother Coleman. A few years after my divorce, we married and God has blessed us.

As I look back over my life, I realize that God had a plan for me. I became complacent and separated myself from God but He never took His hands off me. The enemy found an opening and entered in. God sees the future. I thank and praise Him that He is a forgiving God. Like the father in the prodigal son, He welcomed me back into a personal relationship with Him, blessed me and healed my broken spirit.

"I MADE A MISTAKE"

    Sometimes we go along each day facing life as if we live on a 30x30 block of Ice moving around and walking with fear beside us. When a good and happy day comes, we wish it would last forever. This is where God comes in. You are the star in "The Life's Play" and given a very positive blessing – <u>LIFE</u>. It's a gift paid for with the blood of Jesus. He gave everything so you can have life more abundantly, so you can be a star in this play.

    There are people who want to end their lives by thinking that "no one's life is as hard as mine". My marriage is broken, a love affair broke up a happy home, I'm homeless, I lost someone by death. I lost my job. I'm sick etc. Look around, there are people dying of Cancer and other ailments. Soldiers are on the front line facing death. So many more people are in different stages in life. These are the one's who hold life as very dear to them.

    I heard on the news where a mother with her three children, drove her car in the river and the reporter said someone heard her call out, "I made a mistake" as she and her children were submerged into the water – **THE COLD RIVER WATER!** Another woman drove her car into a lake but she survived and she called out that she had made a mistake too.

    When you try to commit suicide all your dreams and hopes are gone. There's no way out of Death. It's all up to you. Check with a church, a police station, a hospital or a friend for help. Someone can get help for you. Someone may be able to point out your potential, your possibilities or your dreams. Don't keep your pain to yourself. Talk to someone. God gave you life to live to the fullness and He gave you a reason for joy. I thank God every day for my life. I ask Him to run my life daily. Every day is a new day with new hopes and new dreams.

Please don't be a person who will say "I've made a mistake", it can't be mended. Please don't throw this gift of life back into God's face. He gave you life from his Heart and you are loved more than you could ever believe or think. **Don't give up!** Whenever you have this feeling, please go to the nearest hospital. Ask to visit the hospice ward. Visit those people who are really dying and want to live.

Above all, take this advice: Please seek Jesus with your whole heart. You will find peace and love. Every day won't be what you want it to be but Jesus will supply your needs. Just ask Him. By the way, when you visit the hospice ward you may run into someone who tried to kill themselves and did not complete the job. They may live but they will suffer for the rest of their life's Bad Mistake.

—Sallie Proctor

BELIEVE GOD AND HAVE FAITH

This is where it all started. I was a 27-year old young lady when I met a man ten years older than me. I thought he would teach me a thing or two but instead, I went to hell and back. I am a strong believer in Jesus Christ and I have a lot of faith. The pastor of my church in Jamaica taught me how to use faith. I love him so much that I gave my son his middle name. I ran to him when I was abused and accused. I was happy to go to church just to hear him preach about faith. When I was going through my abuse I prayed to God and remembered what my pastor said about faith.

I met this man in 1986. We lived together and had one child. I married him in 1992. It was then I became pregnant with my second child and I was still being abused. His mother, brothers and sisters didn't like me. They busted my head and I got seven stitches. When I got my head busted my pastor said,"Do you want the church lawyer?" I said, "no because I can't fight this battle by myself, it's the Lord's". I forgave him and went back. We had two more children because I believed that God would do something in my life. People told me to leave him, that he is no good, but I still stayed with him and put my trust in God.

In 2003 his mother wanted to take him and my children along with her to the United States. They wanted to leave me back home so they could send someone to the house to hurt me again. I told my pastor and he said, "he isn't going to the U.S.

and leave you here". We prayed about it and here I am in the U.S. with my four children.

When he came here he stayed with his mom for three months and she put him out on the street. Then he went to live at his sister's house and she put him out on the street. At this time I was living in NJ with one of my children. I took him in because he was my husband and the rest of the children were with him. He wanted to come to my home and abuse me the same way he was doing back home. I said, "NO WAY". I put him out too!

During our time together he had said to me once that the children were not his, which was a lie because I had never been with anyone else. We had nothing to do with each other during this time. He said, "You do what you want to do. I don't care". Still abusing me he went and told my family he wanted the marriage to work and that I didn't want it to work. My cousin tried to talk me into staying with him and I said no because he was a lion in the house and a lamb on the road. I waited for him to change and he did not. He went to church so someone would believe he was changed. If I needed money, I had to sign a receipt that he had given me some.

I found a lawyer and went to court for a divorce and to get my children. One of my cousins said, "what if he becomes a bum and doesn't want to take care of the children? I said, "God will take care of them". It has been almost two years now and I don't get anything from him. My kids are fine, growing up good, active in the church and doing well in school because I said God would take care of them and I believed it by faith.

My husband is presently in prison for something he did wrong on his job. His mother is dead. I am well and so are my children. So the story goes, Believe God, Have Faith and God can fix any problem.

I believe God will send someone to love my children and me and treat us with respect.

—Anonymous

WISDOM THAT COMES FROM GOD

It was a beautiful spring day. Bright sunlight streamed down from a clear blue sky and danced upon the flecks of morning dew that coated our front yard. A small batch of flowers had just begun to come to life in our front yard and the warm burst of red and yellow was a welcome sight after such a cold, hard winter. The house that we lived in was a large two-story frame house, which sat off of a lonely dirt road. Age and harsh weather had taken its toll leaving the walls a dull grayish-brown color with only a few flecks of the original white paint remaining.

My sister Rebecca was six years old and I was nine. Like most young girls we were restless and full of energy. On that morning my mother was out front doing chores and we were running around the house looking for something to occupy our time. After a few less interesting ideas were voted down I suggested, "Why not pretend that we're having a tea party?" We immediately knew we had to dress up for such an important event, so we rushed to my mother's closet. My sister chose a beautiful floral dress, a pair of black high heel shoes and my mother's favorite mink stole. I decided on a red dress, brown shoes and a matching pocket book. Dressed and ready to go, we went to the kitchen to start the party.

Our kitchen was a drab; empty room with well-worn floors, a wobbly dining set and a huge black potbelly stove that's crackling orange flame was all we had to keep us warm. We searched the room for food to serve at our party. Unfortunately the cupboards were bare. The only thing we could find to eat was a bowl of unshelled peanuts on the kitchen table. Not much perhaps, however in our imaginations we'd stumbled onto a feast. Our party was about to begin.

Using paper napkins as our plates and the teacups from our play set, we prepared the table. We had so much fun as we talked, laughed and ate our peanuts. Once the party was over we hurried to clean up before my mother came back inside from her yard work. My sister collected all of her shells and placed them in the bottom of her dress. But as she walked to the stove to discard them she got too close and her dress caught fire. Before we knew it my mother's fur stole was also ablaze. I tried to smother the flames by beating them with a dishtowel but I only made things worse. My sister was engulfed in flames.

Fortunately, my mother, father and uncle were out in the front yard and heard our cries for help. By the time they came inside my sister was badly burned. I watched helplessly as they rushed her out to the car. My nine-year-old mind could not comprehend why such a horrible thing had happened. I can still remember how devastated I was.

The doctors told my parents that Rebecca's condition was life threatening. She was admitted immediately with severe burns that covered both of her thighs and her entire stomach. Each day that passed bought such sadness as I truly missed my sister and somehow felt that I was to blame for what had happened to her. My mother and father would visit her each day, but because of my age I was unable to go. She endured long and painful treatments where she was forced to sit in water as hot as she could stand it to remove the dead skin that covered her body. The doctors informed my parents that Rebecca needed skin grafting operations to repair the damage. However my parents had no money to pay for the procedure. After six weeks the hospital decided to send her home. There was nothing else they could do.

My mother and father were very religious and taught us about God at an early age. Every Sunday morning before breakfast we gathered around the table for prayer, scripture and a song. My seven brothers and sisters and I were each required learning a bible verse and reciting it during our prayer meeting. My parents believed in the power of prayer. Well now they had an opportunity to test their faith. Would God answer them?

When Rebecca arrived home, her burns were still raw and incredibly sensitive. She was in such pain. My father was a very strong man but this was even more than he could bear. My father knew that raising the money for the grafting operation would be almost impossible so he did the only thing he could. He prayed. Soon after that God spoke to him. He was given (through the Spirit) a natural solution to fix this problem. He collected sap that flowed from the trees in the woods behind our house. He placed the sap on a towel out on our back porch and allowed it to dry before beating it into a powder. Then he sprinkled the powder onto my sister's burns. After a month or so of this daily ritual a miraculous thing happened. My sister's burns began to dry up and heal. My father took my sister back to the hospital for a checkup and they couldn't believe her improvement. God had answered the family's prayer and saved my sister.

My sister survived this tragic accident and grew into an amazing woman. She and I married brothers and collectively have seven children. The double first cousins are very close today. I am happy to say God's wisdom always supersedes man's knowledge. This Godly wisdom given to my father kept my best friend alive. Thanks to that wisdom, my sister and I still have our tea parties today and they're just as much fun as they were all those years ago. I don't know how my life would have turned out if I had lost my sister and best friend. I only know that God knew I needed her here with me.

MY STORY

I was speaking with a friend a while ago on the telephone. He had just become a youth minister in Mississippi after spending several years in the United States Air Force. He was a fraternity brother from my college days. We knew each other well and how we had behaved in school. It was amazing to me that we were discussing spiritual things. I had just been ordained as a deacon at my church. I told him that we needed to get together sometime so that I could tell him what had transpired in my life since I last saw him. He chuckled a little and said, "Everybody has a story".

My story begins November 1, 1957 in Albany New York, the day I was born. I would find out twenty years later that this is where I was adopted by Frances and Charles Jones. They raised me and will always be my mother and father. I remember seeing my mother bring my sister Charlene down the stairs at Christmastime. She was also adopted. At the time, she looked like a little china doll. I was raised in a loving household and my early memories of my father were that he doted on us and loved us very much. My father passed away when I was six years old. His passing left in me an emptiness that would follow me for many years. I loved my mother and sister, but I yearned for a father or at least an older brother that I could talk to. Someone I could talk to about things that bothered me. I could ask him questions my mother and sister couldn't or wouldn't answer. I found out later that I did indeed have a Father I could call on for guidance and direction. He was there all the time waiting for me to call on Him.

I grew up in Schenectady New York. Schenectady was once called "The City that Lights the World" because of General Electric. G.E. controlled the economic and political character of Schenectady. The size of its facilities was almost a city within itself. In school it was generally expected that graduates would do one of three things after high school. Go away to college, join the armed services or get a job at G.E. These days most of G.E. has moved away and the city is known more as a place of drugs and prostitution. It is almost embarrassing to tell someone familiar with the area that you are from Schenectady.

My neighborhood was comprised of several different ethnic groups. Besides my family, there was only one other black family. Most of my neighbors were Polish. Because of my surroundings and the fact that Schenectady is in an area that's hit with freezing cold and heavy snowfall during the winter months, I learned to play all types of sports. I learned to ice skate and to play hockey. I excelled at basketball and football, which I learned to play in my neighborhood. It is because of this background that I learned at an early age to appreciate people for their differences. Although we liked different types of music or had different views on social issues, we respected one another for who we were and not what we were.

The Bible says **"Train up a child in the way he should go: and when he is old, he will not depart from it"** (Prov. 22:6). I started attending church at an early age. I was baptized and attended Emmanuel Baptist Church. I served as an usher and participated in their youth group. I played basketball on the church's team and when it was time to go away to college, I received a scholarship from them. My family was the only black family in the church. Most of the other families lived in the suburbs and their children attended schools where they lived. I went to the local Boy's Club, which was predominantly black, but I felt separated from the other kids there because I lived on the other side of town. In some ways this made me feel as though I was not really connected to them. At the same time it opened up a world to me that I might not have otherwise known existed. We were not poor, but by no means were we rich. Being around successful people inspired me to want to be successful. They were in many ways my role models and what I aspired to be.

My social life outside of school sports and neighborhood friends, revolved around the church. They gave me the opportunity to travel with them. We attended conferences across the country. I was a delegate to the New York Baptist Youth Convention for several years. I became known for my involvement in various charitable events that gave me the opportunity to serve on the board of the NY State Baptist Youth Convention during my senior year in high school. The Lord was with me and I was totally involved. I even considered going to Oral Roberts University but decided that Tulsa, Oklahoma was just a little too far away. I had discovered that I had talent as an artist and I set my sights on attending art school. I felt the Lord was blessing me and answering all my prayers.

In truth, even though I was doing all this, I still had not really developed a personal relationship with Jesus. Following graduation from high school, I headed off to college and my life would never be the same. I went to Southampton College in Long Island, NY in the fall of 1975 to study art. I had no real fear about being away from home. Through my travels with my family and church I became accustomed to being away from home and on my own. Throughout high school, church was my life and now I was entering a world filled with many things I had never experienced. I had never been to any dancing parties and now on the first night of college I was at one. I had not done drugs, didn't drink or have sex. I was being accepted and I slowly started to adapt to my new environment. I became enamored with those things that were not previously part of my life.

I was growing up, but not spiritually. I was leaving behind all the values and teachings that had blessed me and kept me as a youth. I was being led, not by the Lord, but by those things that were sinful and contrary to His way. I chose to leave Southampton after one year to transfer to Rochester Institute of Technology. I felt that they had a better Art Department that would offer me more opportunities upon graduation. Still, I was lost in those things that are of the flesh. I become bored with art and in my immaturity I decided it wasn't fun anymore. I eventually changed to Business Administration with the goal of a career in Advertising.

I did well in marketing courses (which interested me) and not so great in others. I became popular on campus and started exhibiting leadership skill. I became a charter member of the first African-American fraternity on campus. The Phi Beta Sigma Fraternity Inc. I was the first chapter President and was known throughout Rochester especially after an appearance on a local TV show. This was heady stuff for a shy guy from upstate New York! In many ways I thought I had it all figured out. I still prayed, but in my freshman year I stopped going to church. Sunday became just a day to recover from Friday and Saturday nights. I was lost and didn't know it. Like many people, I was skating on thin ice and I was about to fall through.

I was twenty-three years old when my mother died and after graduation my fiancé and I relocated to Houston, Texas where I was employed as a District Manager for the Houston Post newspaper. I was doing well. My sister was married and making a life for herself in Pennsylvania. Now everything was about to change. Two years before she died, my mother informed us that we were both adopted and that we had different parents. At the time it didn't mean much to me. This was my mother. The only one I had ever known and my sister was my sister. I was devastated by mother's death. I felt alone in the universe. Now the fact that I was adopted led me to despair. I was alone. I asked myself how it could be possible that anyone really loved me if my own birth mother didn't want me? My feeling of self-worth was gone. It destroyed my relationship with my fiancé and with other women for years to come.

I broke up with my fiancé and moved back to Schenectady for a short while. Then I moved to Pennsylvania with my sister and finally ended up in New York City. I was lost. I started doing drugs heavily and using women to make myself feel good. I made bad choices and this led to a failed marriage and to the birth of two children with women that I wasn't married to.

I recognized two things about myself at an early age. The first is that I have always had a sense that I am going to do something special in my life. I didn't know what it would be or when it would happen. It's just something that has always been with me and something I could never really explain. It was a feeling that God was going to do something special in my life that would glorify Him. Even when I was going through the worst times in my life, I have always had the feeling that I wasn't meant to be in that situation. No matter where I found myself at any particular moment, I knew it was not the end. God would not leave me this way; he had something more for me to do.

The second thing I recognized is that I have always felt that I am somewhat apart from the crowd. This has had both a positive and negative effect on my life. I have been able to travel in different circles and I have always been comfortable with different types of people and various settings. At the same time I have developed few close friendships. My new wife is my best earthly friend. I am, I believe, what one of my good friends once called me, a loner. I love people and work in a position where I interact with people on a daily basis. I have a desire to help others and to get to know them but there is always a part of me that I keep to myself. I really do enjoy my own company at times. I appreciate having time alone to reflect and talk with the Lord. I am a shy person by nature, so the fact that I am able to speak before a gathering of people amazes me. I am compelled to share the Word of God. Speaking before the congregation takes me totally out of my comfort zone. That is why I know this isn't of or about me. Left on my own, I would run to the back of the church. I can't turn back no matter what. I will preach the Word of God. I don't know why He chose me. I certainly don't feel worthy but I will do all that I can to be what He would have me to be.

Where the Lord leads, I will follow. I believe everything that has transpired in my life has led me to where I am. ***Romans 8:28 states, "And we know that all things work together for good to them that love God, to them who are the called according to His purpose".*** I have come to realize that I have a Father who has guided me and looked after me all of my life. I stated before that I always knew that I would do something special in my life. I now realize that there is nothing more special or important than winning souls for the Lord.

—E. Jones

WILL YOU PLAY CATCH WITH ME?

There is no confidence like confidence that comes from the Lord. "Have a little talk with Jesus and He will make everything alright". Just a little talk—this is all the Lord needs to help us.

I remember my first full day of being on campus at Colgate-Rochester/Crozer Divinity School in the summer of 2000. I wanted to be there before the beginning of the fall semester so that I could get started on what I had been secretly dreaming about for a long time. I figured that God would miraculously work everything out for me without any obstacles.

So there I was walking onto a luscious green lawn towards the seminary when students walked out of the central building on their last day of a summer class about God and American Baseball. They came out to play catch and were excited to see and chat with me. They wanted to know if I was going to be a great student. At the time, there were misconceptions going back and forth about me in contradictory ways. One rumor indicated that as a Phi Beta Kappa undergraduate, I was one of the best scholars around (that was 5 years ago and quite distant from whom I had become). Another rumor was that since I had earned mediocre grades at the University of Chicago Law School, I could never be more than a mediocre student in Seminary. I was quite proud of being even a mediocre graduate from the #2 law school in the country. No one had it right about me at a time when I desperately wanted to be understood and to understand the calling on my life.

The game of catch grabbed my attention. Even though I played baseball in high school, I was suddenly intimidated by the talented interchange taking place in front of me. Balls were going back and forth at amazing speeds; 50, 60 maybe even 70 miles an hour. These guys and gals were very good. They were better than I had ever been. As I thought about trying to play catch with them on an equal level, I reminded myself that I didn't have the money for a baseball glove.

I watched them as the ball went back and forth, back and forth. All of a sudden the class professor Dr William Herzog II walked up beside me and began to talk in my ear like a baseball coach. I was impressed that he even had anything to say to me. "Son", he said, "your field is in the classroom. The classroom is going to be your baseball field. Play baseball in the classroom".

Fall came and orientation was inspiring. Seminary classes opened and I had signed up for the hardest possible load that a first-year student could take. I was going to jump into the Old Testament, the New Testament, Hebrew, Greek and African American Women's studies while working two to three jobs on campus. The workload itself was enough to make one panic and in light of everything else that I had to do, a simple 20 page reading assignment would make my heart pound in fear. I had fear of not doing well.

Even though I had been taught the bible, my biggest surprise was that I really knew nothing about theological education. Throughout my childhood, my mother had been the Superintendent of The Rose of Sharon Community Church's Sunday School. She faithfully prepared before teaching her classes. Her motto was that if she was going to teach anything to other parents' children, my brother and I were going to know it first.

I had three Sunday Schools as a child. Saturday night (in preparation for actual Sunday School), Sunday School itself, with the nicest teachers in the world and then after-church Bible Study where my mother would read all types of materials. She even read adult historical Christian fiction novels to us. We also read and talked about the Bible every night of the week. If you talk to my mother about teaching Sunday School, she will tell you that her only strength was in being a disciplined teacher but she was more than that. Mother was a devoted teacher and I spent hours upon hours where I loved to see her in love with God and his Word. My mother sang and cried and prayed and sought the Lord during the hours my brother and I spent with her.

Not only did I not know anything about theological education, more than anything I had never been exposed to theological debates that had dominated classroom discussions. It was impossible for me to know which theories were legitimate and which ones weren't in the matter of days. I began to understand the tensions in the Biblical test for Women in ministry while at the same time trying to figure out why it was important for some professors to believe that Jesus did not perform the miracles told to us in the Gospels.

Mechanically, seminary work also seemed to challenge me beyond my capabilities. My first New Testament assignment on a passage of scripture required me to render my own original interpretation from the Greek text. How was I supposed to read Greek on my first day of class? I didn't know then that there were several ways to assert translations of Greek without even understanding the Greek alphabet. So I was pretty lost. I promised myself that I would champion my work in seminary. I also promised myself that I would be excellent at everything I did. So then because I didn't know how to excel, I didn't complete one single written assignment. I just watched everything and took in what my classmates did. I just watched and failed every class except for the teacher who angered me by giving me a "C" when I hadn't completed any work.

That winter, I briefly took on a job in the field of law that was way over my head. I only mention it to say that I believe the Lord showed me that job to present things for the future that were way beyond my understanding. Also to understand my place in the job, I repeatedly called a woman I liked to see if she could encourage me through this position and guide me along the way. She never tried to help and I waited on her like Charlie Brown waited for the Great Pumpkin. I believe that somebody besides me will wait on someone to rescue him or her from places where only the Lord's hands will reach. I seriously and deeply waited for her to rescue me. I wanted teachers to rescue me and encourage me and they wouldn't, fellow students didn't utter a word and excluded me from the best of their conversations. I wasn't comfortless though. I just wasn't receiving the comfort and direction from other people that I thought I could substitute for the Lord. For indeed I remember Rev. Linda Evans prophesying that I would be a New Testament Scholar someday. I remember Ms. Clesether Young prophesying that I would serve the Lord in many professional fields. I remember the Church of Love Faith Center bus driver Darryl telling me not to be afraid of the ministry before me.

That spring, the school made my re-entrance to Seminary as easy as filling out another application. There was one thing missing though. On my way home from a long walk in Rochester, a voice came to me and said, "Play catch with me. Why don't you play catch with me?" I knew it was the Lord and I skipped with joy the fifty yards or so home. God said that he would play catch with me. Since then every bit of theology and every bit of Biblical Study and every bit of ministry has been as simple and direct as playing catch with God. From that day to this, I have never had a problem connecting to God over a theological assignment. When I am in class, the Lord shows up and everything enters a different dimension in both how I see my professors and in how I understand God's Word.

I have some wonderful stories to share about how the Lord has spoken to me in seminary and even more of the Lord's work is being written on my heart right now. At Rose of Sharon Community Church, Mr. Jones sang a song called "Have a Little Talk with Jesus". Just a <u>little</u> talk will change your life. One <u>little</u> talk with the Lord will make everything brand new. That's all it takes – one little talk.

"Will you play catch with me? Why don't you play catch with me?"

—Tobias Pinckney

MY CHILDHOOD MEMORIES

My childhood memories start when I was three years old and consist of the time when my father was in prison. The day he came home I remember waiting in the yard, looking up the road in the direction my mom told me he would be coming from. He was wearing overalls and a denim cap. He brought me a yellow, red and green light made from toothbrushes.

While daddy was away, mom worked for two or three Caucasian families who did not pay her the salary that she deserved, but they always gave her plenty of food. That meant we ate well. The families she worked for also gave her plenty of clothes. After he got home everything changed because he was an evil nasty person. Daddy was a miserable person most of the time and he made sure his family experienced part of his misery by hitting you just because he was your daddy and he felt that he could. He didn't care what he hit you with, whether it was a broom handle, a stick or his fist. Mom wasn't for a lot of hugs and kisses either but at least you knew you were loved. I never saw him hit mom, but he would call her every nasty curse he could think of. I saw her many days going to another room to cry. My oldest brother O.T. would never say anything to him regardless of how nasty he got, but Lowell and James would let him know they did not like the way he treated mommy. One day James let daddy know exactly how he felt, so my father thought it was time for him to let James know that he wasn't going to stand for James telling him what to do. Daddy started towards the house to get the shotgun to shoot him. I heard him when he said, "I will shut your mouth for good". I out ran my father to the house and got the gun. I gave it to my brother Lowell who was working in the back of the house. James didn't get shot that day, but I got the beating of my life!

Each Sunday we had to go to Sunday school, but on the fourth Sunday of the month we attended Church service. This was because most members of the church were too poor to put an offering in the collection plate to pay the Minister a salary so he went to a different church each Sunday to preach. All of the churches would pay him what they were able to pay and give him donations of food from their gardens and farms to take to his family.

We lived in a house on the land where daddy worked as a sharecropper for Mr. J.T. Fuller. Sometimes when it rained, we needed an umbrella inside the house and we had to put buckets around to catch the water that leaked from the tin-topped roof. The house was so ragged that we didn't want anyone to visit. I was always embarrassed when anyone would come to visit because we never had nice furniture and thought our house was the worse house in the community. I had five brothers and two sisters. The first eleven years of my life there were only five of us (3 boys and 2 girls). Years later there were two more brothers and another sister. The first five of us caught a hard way to go and were tormented on the farm. We had to work eight to ten hours a day. Sometimes dad would wake us up at 4:00 a.m. It would be so dark that we couldn't see in order to do any work, so we would sit and look at one another until daylight.

We raised corn, peanuts, yams, watermelons, cantaloupes, cucumbers, black-eyed peas, butter beans, string beans, white potatoes, collard greens, cabbage, beets, squash, cotton and hogs. The hogs were killed in the winter and the meat from the hogs was kept in a room called the smoke house. The side of the hog (which was the bacon) would be packed in boxes with layers of salt to preserve it and the shoulders and hams would be hung and smoked. In late November or the first week of December, we raised sugar cane. We made syrup by taking stalks of cane and extracting the juice from them by putting them into a machine pulled by mules. Then the juice was boiled in a big pot until it became syrup. The syrup was poured into jars or big cans to be used later or to be sold. When the cotton was ready to be picked, everyone else would make cotton-picking sacks to fit the size of the person, but not good old daddy. He gave all of us adult sized sacks that you weren't allowed to empty until it was full. Sometimes my back would ache so bad that I couldn't fall asleep for the first two or three hours at bedtime.

We would always have one of the first gardens to have vegetables ready to eat. We would share it with many of the neighbors and also with some of the families that my mother worked for. The only thing that made me angry about the sharing was that my brother Lowell and I would have to take the vegetables to white families. We said if all of the black neighbors could come and get whatever mom was giving them, we felt that they should do the same. We thought it only fair because they had cars and trucks and all of their children could drive. When we went to take the vegetables to any white family's house, we had to enter through the back door. Lowell and I said if the vegetables we raised were good enough for them to eat, then we should be good enough to go through the front door. And that is exactly what we did! We didn't have every day shoes, we only had "Sunday shoes" to wear to church and it had rained the day before we delivered the vegetables. We felt really good going through the front door tracking mud all the way to the kitchen. Our great aunt Miller was their cook and housekeeper. She came straight from work to our house to tell mommy what we did and we were scolded, so we didn't do that again, but it sure felt good to us for that one time because I always felt that I was just as good as them, and it was wrong to be treated that way.

The saddest part of farming was the way we farmed. My good old dad thought he was the smartest man that ever pooped. He was so dumb that he didn't even know it. He had talents. He was a good carpenter and could lay bricks, but business wise he didn't have a clue. My mother begged him to rent the land that we worked, which meant we would have a paid asset for half of the land. Oh no! good old Bennie wasn't renting land when he could work both halves. The meant that Mr. Fuller got half of everything we raised. Therefore the expenses for fertilizer, feeding the animals and buying anything else that was needed came out of our half.

When I was a teenager, I remember the leaves changing colors. Some were a little green, some yellow and brown, letting us know that it was time to go into the field to pick peas. On this particular day, I recall almost being bitten by a rattlesnake. Snakes are able to blend in well with the dirt, crops and grass. No one had ever explained to me how a rattlesnake would coil itself into a circle and start rattling just before it was ready to bite. I heard the snake rattling and I didn't know what the noise was but daddy did. I remember his words so well. He said, "Willia Mae! Don't move." He said it in a voice that I had never heard from him before. He ran, got a big stick and killed the snake. That is one good thing my father did for me. Ever since that day I have had a great fear of snakes. After I was grown with children, whenever we would go to the zoo, I wouldn't go into the room where the snakes were. I was only able to conquer my fear by forcing myself to walk through the room with the snakes and asking my husband Claude to hold my hand and walk on the side where the snakes were. When I exited the room I felt uncomfortable, but not afraid.

I used to pray that I could have a birthday twice a year so I could hurry up and become eighteen so I could leave home. I always knew that life had more to offer and regardless of how black you were you deserved the best. That included a decent place to live, a good job and more importantly a good education. Most black people where I was growing up didn't think that education was important. White people didn't want us to get an education at all. The school year was only six months long but most of the black children went for three months or less. Most of the black boys dropped out after they finished the fourth or fifth grade. Some never went to school at all. As for me, I always said that I would go to college. I got married at the age of eighteen in Selma Alabama. We moved to Staten Island, N.Y. when I was nineteen years old and my husband and I had no desire to become farmers. We wanted our children to have a better life than ours. My biggest dream was to have a family and to see my children have a better life than I had. I always had hope and belief in God. God blessed me to see my dream come true for my children and grandchildren. At the age of forty-four, I was blessed to go to Staten Island Community College and got an Associates Degree in Childcare.

My mother was a prayer warrior. And she taught me to put God first in your life and set goals for yourself. I am currently eighty years old and I am still praying and putting God first. I believe in studying the Bible and applying it to your daily living. My favorite scripture is Ephesians 6:6 and in order to serve God you have to move yourself out of the way. I have been on the battlefield for God since I was 12 years old and I am a blessed, happy, mother, grandmother and great-grandmother.

I am blessed and happy!!!
Remember:
Only what you do for Christ will last
And
Whatever you do that is good,
Work to make it better
Then
Whatever you do that is better,
Keep working until it is your best!

— WILLIA MAE EDWARDS

EDUCATION: KEY TO A SUCCESSFUL LIFE

    First and foremost, always keep God in all of your decision-making. He does not leave us alone to bear life's trials and tribulations. Secondly, I have one key word for future generations, Education! Not only academic achievement, while it is indeed paramount, but learning in all aspects of life. If I had the chance to relive life again, here is how it would unfold and is my advice to younger generations. As an adolescent I would sit at the feet of my elders and soak up their life lessons, truly listening this time around. Elder generations are a wealth of knowledge simply because they have already experienced many of the issues younger generations have yet to endure. They possess wisdom; insight to living that may well be a positive life-changing source for generations following.

    Yes, I would learn those scratch recipes for making homemade biscuits, yeast rolls, and cakes. In hindsight, much of these ingredients included items that were staples in the home, flour, eggs, butter, milk, sugar, yeast and spices. This was an economical way to stretch the budget in hard times back in the day and could aid in getting through a "rainy" season in today's world. Also there was something about the number of punches to the yeast dough, how much cold butter to cut into flour for the biscuits or adding a little bit of "this and that" to the cake batter that was paramount to the positive outcome. The sanguine take-away would have been to pass those nuances on to the younger generations. They make great memories and the taste of homemade food is hard to beat.

While saturating my inner essence in the life lessons of my elders, I would also immerse my mind in academia studies. Being a learned student in all areas of education is important but next time around I would concentrate on excelling in my passion for a working career (for me writing). A qualified, trustworthy mentor(s) in your field of choice with like passion to hone your skills is a great opportunity and doesn't cost anything by time well spent. As you glean information, write it down. Journaling is a great way to accumulate valuable life notes. It will also tell you how much and in what areas you have progressed. Don't be afraid to ask questions of your teachers, scholars and those that can provide life lessons. If you never question, how can your learn? There is no reason to meander through life in an unquestioning stupor, especially in today's world with all manner of social media just a mouse click away. If you don't have access to a computer at home, make use of the computers at your local library.

Set realistic goals, attainable for the short and long-term prior to high school graduation. Review your goals each week to ensure you are staying on track towards your objective. Let nothing detain you from what God has given you to do with the natural gift(s) that He has bestowed on you to carry out. If someone tells you "you'll never do that or you'll never make it" or any such similarity, pray for that person and love them from afar. Obviously they do not have your best interest at heart. Surround yourself with people who are optimistic, those that see the glass as being half full instead of half empty.

Socialize to the extent that it does not distract you from your goals and dreams. After obtaining your college degree(s), technical trade license(s), etc. there will be plenty of time to spread your social wings. You will have your entire life to work in a successful field or own your own business. Always have a Plan "B" in case the road gets bumpy and your Plan "A" becomes unattainable for a season. However, when you have attained your goals, or even before, always reach back and mentor others. Finally, give God all of the glory, and all of the praise for what He has done in your life. God Bless.

—CINDY WILLIAMS NEWSOME
Author of *Hobbstown: The Forgotten Legacy of a Unique African American Community* and *The Vain Girl*

©2011 *Education: Key to a Successful Life*

WHAT OUR YOUTH NEED

"What do our youth need?" It's a question we hear everywhere. As a mother and grandmother, I have a genuine concern for the temptations and struggles that our young people are facing today. There have been so many magazines, books and TV talk show discussions about the challenges that teens and young adults face from addictions to drugs and alcohol, sexual promiscuity at increasingly younger ages, to gang affiliation leading to illegal activity ranging from robbery and drug dealing all the way to murder. Young men and women under the age of twenty five are among the largest segment of our population suffering from chronic depression.

So what is the cure for what ails this crucial segment of the population? Parents, grandparents, youth organizations and churches throughout the world are searching for an answer. Many churches and social youth agencies are spending millions of dollars to create programs and activities to "keep kids off the streets". These programs may be missing the real problem. Even with the involvement of organizations that have well-developed youth programs, it does not guarantee that the young people are getting what they need. The fact is our youth may not need a "program"; they may simply need someone to sit down and listen to them.

In short, our young people need a hand. They need adults who care about them and are concerned with their needs. They need to establish reliable relationships with people who not only talk about doing what is right, but who lead by example. They need to be invited by older adults/mentors to explore their spirituality and to develop a relationship with God. Mature adults have the life experience that this group lacks. They are often wiser in ways of the spiritual journey. Older people need to share this wisdom with young adults and be prepared to listen to their experiences and challenge themselves to really put themselves in the shoes of these young men and women. For example, I like to refer to one of my favorite verses which states: "Train up a child in the way he should go: and when he is old, he will not depart from it". This verse says to me that programs cannot replace good parenting and the way God wants our youth to live. Our youth needs to be restored to the right relationship between God, man and among humankind. Parents must start when children are in their formative years, and make a real effort to provide a loving and supportive home environment, and act themselves as positive role models. I've learned from listening and learning from my own children and grandchildren that our youth needs to be loved. If they feel ignored, misunderstood or disconnected from parents, guardians or other family, the lack of acceptance and love will often cause them to seek people who can fill this void.

Parents should monitor what their children are watching with a specific emphasis on both television programs, its content as well as the advertisements. Young people are impressionable and advertising leads them to believe that their wants and needs can be fulfilled by purchasing items. Cars, clothing, jewelry and even soft drinks are constantly placed in front of young people on their favorite programs tying "coolness" to these items. Young adults often feel pressure to buy these items to keep up with the latest trends. This influence can keep them out of touch with their deepest needs and desires. It often times leads them to disappointment, disillusionment and even hopelessness when they don't find happiness for fulfillment after attaining the objects of their desire. With the help of the right adult, they may find that these items are nothing more than distractions from what they desire most; the sense of belonging, identity and intimacy that we find when we are connected with God.

Ultimately our youth needs to see living, breathing examples of adults who have made choices and commitments and the solid, fulfilling lives these decisions have brought them, offering their skills and insights along the way. In a word, our youth needs you. Step up today and become a real part of a young person's life. You'll be surprised what a blessing it will be to you both.

—MADELINE EVANS

I AM BECOMING THE WOMAN THAT HE WANTS ME TO BE

Proverbs 22:6 tells us, "Train up a child in the way he should go: and when he is old, he will not depart from it. I give God honor and praise for what He has done for me especially through the rough times. At some point in our lives many of us have lost things that are dear to us. Psalm 86:6-7 says, "When they walk through the valley weeping… they will continue to grow stronger.

When I was a young wife at 22 my husband left and went back home to live with his mom. During this time I went through five states of grief.

1. Denial: God, it can't be happening!
2. Anger: God why are you permitting this to happen to me? At least I got married and didn't shack up.
3. Bargaining: I asked God to let it only be a dream and let it go away.
4. Depression: When it didn't go away, I went into silent withdrawal. I didn't want to have anything to do with God and I got lukewarm. God's Word says if I am lukewarm, He will spit me out of His mouth.
5. Acceptance: I got to the area in my life when I said, "Not my will, but thy will be done."

After that, things started to change in my life. By turning my life over to God, He gave me the grace to release, embrace, grieve and become stronger. As I prayed, I got into God's Word. I am becoming the woman that He wants me to be.

—Rev. Washington

LET IT GO

> *"Brethren I count not myself to have apprehended; but this one thing I do, forgetting those things which are behind, and reaching forth unto those things which are before, I press toward the mark for the prize of the high calling of God in Christ Jesus."*
> — Phil 3:13-14

We often find ourselves looking back over our lives, reminiscing about the "good old days", if you will. We remember when we were children – the times we would sneak out when we were told not to go away from the house. The times we would sneak down to the brook when we were told not to, and had fun just throwing stones into the water, or perhaps, jump into the water even though we were told not to go swimming and then mommy would find out and we'd get into trouble. Maybe, you had a best friend, and the two of you would get together and tell each other secrets. But then, you remember that best friend told everybody else what you said. Then you realize those "good old days" weren't so good after all.

Potpourri From The Heart

*"Remember ye not the former things,
neither consider the things of old.
Behold, I will do a new thing: now it
shall spring forth; shall ye not know it?
I will even make a way in the wilderness,
and rivers in the desert."*
— Isa. 43:18-19

    Sometimes we dwell too long on things that have happened to us in the past. We find that we remember all of the bad things that have happened in our lives. We sit for hours just thinking about people in the past who have hurt us in one way or another. We remember how we used to get a beating for something that brother did. We remember the times we got whipped on account of something sister said. We find that we remember how cousin Lessie came by and borrowed twenty-five dollars from us and never paid it back. We think about the time Uncle Jim borrowed the car and got into an accident and dented it, then tried to say that the dent was already there. We begin to think about how sometimes we got our feelings hurt for no reason. We found that people we thought we could trust turned around and lied on us. Some things we have a hard time forgetting.

    Then, there are times when we try to do what's right, and find that we are ostracized and criticized. We try to do good, and someone turns it around for evil. We lend a so-called friend money and they never repay it. We try to be there for others but who's there for us? Sometimes you go to church where you are sure to find peace and love but you hear so much arguing, bickering and backbiting that you don't even want to go back anymore. Seems like there's no love or peace anywhere. Lord have mercy!

    But God is saying it's time to **"LET IT GO"**. It's time to let go of those things that have happened in the past. All those hurts: give them to Jesus. All of those disappointments, give them to Jesus. All the tears you've cried because of people mistreating you, and despitefully using you, give them to Jesus. Paul said,

"Forgetting those things that are behind, I'm reaching forth unto those things which are before." It's time for us to reach forth and press towards the goal of eternal life. For the Bible says, "It's appointed unto man once to die, and after that the judgment." It's time to lay aside every weight" – everything that hinders you from being the man or woman that God means for you to be. Anything that keeps you from accepting Christ as your personal savior, anything that keeps you from reading your bible, anything that hinders you from getting a prayer through, God is saying to **"LET IT GO"**.

We've gotten so used to dwelling on the troubles of the past; we've become so comfortable remembering the disappointments and failures of yesterday that we don't even realize that bitterness has crept into our hearts. We have held onto these hurts for so long that we've gotten quite comfortable with them, and we're being crushed under the weight of them and we don't even realize it. We find it hard to throw old baggage away even though it is dragging us down. Well this is a new day, and it's time for a change. Its time for you to move on with your life. God said in Isaiah 43:18,19: "*Remember ye not the former things,* (forget about them) *neither consider the things of old* (don't even think about them). *Behold, I will do a new thing; now it shall spring forth;* (He's going to do something He's not done for you before, right now) *shall ye not know it?* (You will be aware of it) *I will even make a way in the wilderness,* (where you cannot see your way, He will make it clear for you to walk) *and rivers in the desert."* (Where your life looks empty and barren, He will make it flourish).

But first God wants you to forget the hurts of the past because He's going to bless you in a new way and you're going to recognize these blessings as they take place. He's going to make a way for you when you don't see your way. He's going to provide for all your needs. First, you have got to **"LET IT GO"**. Make room for your blessings. Clear the anger from your heart. You've got to begin by forgiving those who have hurt you. The Bible says, "If I regard the iniquity in my heart, the Lord will not hear me". In other words, if I hold anger, bitterness or hatred in my heart, God will not hear my prayers. When Jesus taught his disciples to pray, He said, "And forgive us our trespasses as we forgive those who trespass against us". Peter asked Jesus on one occasion "Lord, when my brother sins against me, how many times shall I forgive him, seven times"? And Jesus answered him, "Until seventy times seven". We cannot even count how many times that God has forgiven us for the wrong things that we have done. He just keeps on forgiving us. Now, it's up to you. If you want the blessings that God has promised, you must be obedient to his Word: first, believe on the Lord Jesus Christ and you shall be saved. Next, repent for holding iniquity in your heart, forgive others and then **"LET IT GO"**. Then you will receive the blessings that God has promised and when God calls you from labor to reward, you will receive eternal life.

—Reverend Dr. Doris J. Gray

Life As Tooth Paste

If you have never seen your life as tooth paste, take a few minutes. What you are about to read in the next few moments might be an awakening introspective reality to you. Perhaps, you are wondering what tooth paste has to do with life. Just before you finish with that thought, think of the time(s) you or someone you know felt like you were being used for whatever reason. May I say to you, life was squeezed out of you like tooth paste being squeezed out of the tube and when the need was no longer there, like the tooth paste, you were tossed.

Using and discarding people as an empty tooth paste tube appears more prominent when individuals wander off from the purpose for which God created them, when individuals they solicit to worldly attractions rather than Godly design and when individuals succumb to worldly pressure for success. The devil's on the loose and targeting young and old people particularly those born to Christian faith. I am sure you would agree with me that there have been a great many individuals who started off as Christians singing in the choir or performing one task or the other in the church, yet for one reason or another they found themselves doing the opposite of what they were taught in churches.

Satan's desire to steal, kill and destroy God's creation has not changed. His primary focus has always been to usurp God's worship and praise and seeks thus of individuals in churches.

His search focuses on talented individuals, particularly in music. Hence, talents that could have been used in the body of Christ are stifled by Satan. It must be understood that Satan's desire for worship emanates from his determination to recapture what he lost, ala music. His desire of worship through music lies in the fact that he was the chief musician until he was dethroned in heaven. Ezekiel has this to say of Satan or Lucifer as he was known prior to descension to Earth, "Thou has been in Eden the garden of God; every precious stone was thy covering, the sardius, topaz, and the diamond, the beryl, the onyx, and the jasper, the sapphire, and the carbuncle, and gold: the workmanship of the tabrets and of thy pipes was prepared in thee in the day that thou was created." (Ezekiel 28:13).

Lucifer as one of the angelic hosts was the chief musician who directed the choir of Heaven. Not only was he able to sing, but God also created him with musical instruments. God is the creator of music. As one listens to Psalms you cannot help but delve in with David as he pours out his heart in worship of God. David said, "He put a new song in my mouth, a hymn of praise to our God. Many will see and fear the LORD and put their trust in him" (Psalm 40:3). It's so disheartening sometimes to observe tragically the latter end of some of the individuals who started well and later found themselves drifted out of churches.

Drifted individuals succumb to worldly lusts promised of the devil. The reality, however, is that Satan has the ability to promise grandeur riches, happiness and satisfaction. He did it to Jesus when he said, "I will give you the kingdoms of this world, if you bow down and worship me" (Matt 4:1-11). Doubtless, Satan continues to make the same promises to individuals today. His ability to dispense some of what he promises is undeniably certain, but not devoid of eternal detriment.

Satan steals lives; he's targeting yours if you let him. He presents you with superfluous offers just to lure you, but refuse the bait. Ultimately Satan's plan is to squeeze life out of you, kill and destroy you in hell. Conversely, God's plan is by far incomparable to what Satan offers. Jeremiah tells us that God's plan is for your good (Jer. 29:11) That plan is tucked away in your DNA. Your DNA has no duplicate; it's unique and full of limitless potentials for success to bring you joy, joy like a river.

Countless squeezed and tossed individuals' lives have been restored as they turned to God. God gives second chances. You'd agree that addiction of any sort, be it alcohol, drugs, prostitution or gambling constitutes some of the ways that Satan squeezes life out of individuals. Unfortunately, Satan only knows how to destroy lives through addictions, but he does not know how to repair. Restoration of destroyed lives is found in Jesus Christ and continues to be available through forgiveness of sin.

Thus, ordinary detergent or whatever cleaning devices one may apply to cleanse people from their sin will not suffice; nothing but the blood of Jesus Christ. The hymn writer says, "What can wash away my sins, nothing but the blood of Jesus…O precious is the flow, that makes me white as snow…" It's only as individuals turn to God are they able to regain all that Satan stole from them. God is gracious! He is the Potter and we are the clay. He alone is able to pick up the broken pieces and put you back like nothing ever happened but you must let Him. We can go to this program and that program and be told that there is a higher power. Well let me tell you that the higher power has a name and it is Jesus! Only His blood can cleanse you from all addictions! What you and I call addiction is simply the ecstasy of Satan's deception. At the inception of the luring to whatever it is that you're addicted to, it felt as though your were walking on cloud nine or realizing it was all an illusion.

Now whatever remains of your fractured life, you have no need to feel worthless or dehumanized from past lifestyles, regrets and sorrows when all you need to do is turn things over to Jesus

Christ. Being the life giver, He is able to restore a life that has been tossed away as that of an empty toothpaste tube and put you on track and give you the enablement to actualizing your potential. As long as the devil did not kill you while he had the chance, it's not too late; as the old saying goes, "Better late than never".

If what has been described in Life As Tooth Paste has touched you in some ways, the intent of this presentation is to inform you that God is the Potter; He gives second chances to those who cry out to Him. You do not have to remain tossed like an empty tube of tooth paste. There is a song in you to sing and a book of your life's journey to write. Don't give up. Thousands, if not millions are waiting to hear your song and read your book! Be blessed in the Lord.

—Rev. Christian Nwakaihe, M-Div.

GREEN BEANS

Green beans, Green beans, not again!
I hate this bitter, sour gem.
They sit on my plate just ready to eat.
Green beans smell worse than a pair of dirty feet.
No one understands what has been done to me
My mom thinks beans are for eternity!
Oh Lord, Oh Lord!
Provide some thing pure and lean.
Please don't make me eat this horrible bean!

—Vernae Taylor

LIFE IS NOT A GAMBLE

Life is filled with questions. Who am I? Why am I here? What do I need to understand? These questions can undermine us throughout our lives. Given an opportunity to infiltrate your mind, they can drag your life into a pit of confusion and fear. Would the answer to these questions bring you comfort? Would they give you direction? Would they bring about a sense of certainty and calm that has eluded you? Give me your attention, for there are answers and they are life-changing.

Mankind's deepest questions are typically asked from a false starting point. They arise because many of us believe in the "element of chance" as a foundational principle. Some people go so far as to assert that chance is the guiding force of their lives – as if such a thing could give guidance. CHANCE does not create anything. Nothing happens by chance. As an individual, you are no accident. You're not a happenstance or a random event; you are masterpiece of art and a special creation of God. There are those who will argue this point with you. They will say, for example, "I won the lottery – that was chance" or "Life is just a game – whatever happens, happens". No! Not true.

Seeing life as random chance or your decisions as just one more bet in a round of roulette is to take a fatalistic view of God's greatest gift, believing that one arrives at their destiny, no matter what. Nothing could be further from the truth. Even our Lord was confronted with the dilemma of this destructive perspective.

Satan tried seducing Jesus Christ to take the short cut of the chance as opposed to fulfilling His divine work. He took Christ to a pinnacle, presenting Him with a vision of the kingdoms of the world and said, "...all of these things I will give to you, if you fall down and worship me...," (Matthew 4:8,9, KJV). All Jesus had to do was forego His understanding of the truth and accept the deadly trap set to derail Him from His purpose in the world. He did not yield because He understood the truth. We have the opportunity to choose certainty and life OVER chance because He made His decision to follow His Father.

Gambling is a pathway to destruction. There is the pedantic, every day version of this destruction to which many can attest. In these scenarios, players lose money, college funds, cars, jewelry, homes and other valuables. This article is not about those kinds of losses, devastating as they may be. It is about the kind of reckless gambling that may cost one their very soul.

When a gambler is "UP", so to speak, they feel the deceptive high of having the whole world in the palm of their hands. They can convince themselves that they can do what they want, when they want and nothing can stop them. Some may be so bold as to say that, "not even God can stop me". The Scripture says, "I can do all things through Christ which strengthens me," (Philippians 4:13, KJV). As you can see, the words of the gambler and the words of the Bible are in direct contradiction. The former is an attitude reflective of rebellion and pride while the latter connotes awareness of one's reliance upon God and their trust in Him for direction along life's journey. Only one course can be correct.

A word of caution – time wasted is irreversible. Gambling on your own self-proclaimed power is time wasted. No doubt, it is a seductive prospect to consider that you hold life's cards and may play them as you see fit. The tactics of the devil rely on this misconception. He will lead you to enjoyment and momentary pleasure in order to entrap you – just as was his plan for our Lord. He takes great pleasure in the thought that you will squander your life. Don't be fooled. There are no pause or rewind buttons in real life. When time passes, it's gone – and gone forever.

The greatest thing we can do with our lives is come to the realization of Christ's great sacrifice on the cross. Christ declared that he came to give life and that, more abundantly. His life and death and resurrection allow us to understand that God created us with a purpose. Jesus died for you and me. What greater evidence could there be that each life is important and has meaning? God sent His only begotten son to die for the sins of the world. This was the supreme expression of love. When He says, "Before you were conceived in your mother's belly, I knew you," (Jeremiah 1:5) it expresses His divine connection with you and His divine Love for you and God cannot lie.

Understanding this, we begin to see how very important it is that we ask Him to reveal His purpose for us to our hearts and minds that we may live our lives in accordance with His plans. Will the Just God who is all good and all loving, yea, the God who knew you before you were even conceived in your mother's womb – will that God not do right? Could you be an accident? Perish the thought! Don't get lost in false ideas about your self-worth – know that your worth comes from the fact that God loves you and wants to bless you with the accomplishment of running life's race in a manner that will leave Him saying, "well done". Take the limitations off of yourself. When feelings of rebellion or rejection appear to taunt you, gravitate to this Scripture from Psalms: "When my father and mother foresake me, then the Lord will take me up" (Psalm 27:10 KVJ).

It is important to dismiss the temptations that are paralyzing your life. This is easier said than done. In fact, you cannot do it – but you can call upon Jesus to do it for you. By asking him, you are deciding to give up on rollling the dice in your earthly walk.

The gambler's life is devoid of true perspective and ultimately filled with regret. Any casino will tell you that if you play long enough, the "house" always wins. In our earthly lives, we may lose money and relationships. In our spiritual walk, the "house" is Satan and his payoff is an empty afterlife, cut off from God. The gambler believes he is his own God. He becomes inflated on the false sense of success and pride borne of momentary victory. God does not bless pride – in His eyes, it is the off-spring of rebellion. It was pride that dethroned Satan when he was counted among God's angels in heaven. Satan gambled on the idea that he was his own God. He has been paying for that errant notion ever since and his ultimate day of reckoning will soon be upon him.

The Word of God details the origin and fall of Satan and, by extension, man's battle with sin, pride and rebellion. The first passage is found in Ezekiel 28:12-19 wherein the creation of a vile and vicious creature named Lucifer is described. Another is Isaiah 14:12-14, where the prophet Isaiah presents the origin and fall of Satan. Based upon these Scriptures (as well as Jude 6, II Peter 2:4 and others) a picture of the fallen angel emerges. Satan was created as one of the host of angelic beings, an anointed cherub, also known as the captain of the cherubic hosts. Sometime prior to the creation of the natural order, Satan's vanity about such things as his beauty and his position, drove his heart to challenge God. As he took up his terrible cause, he was able to secure a considerable following among the angels. The result: the entire lot of them were expelled from Heaven (Luke 10:18, II Peter 2:4, Jude 6, Revelation 12:4). Since that moment, Satan has devoted himself to opposing God in every way possible and destroying all of the good that God has created in the natural order. Satan will be allowed to continue in his course for a time (and for God's purposes), but he will ultimately be confined to Hell for eternity (Revelation 20:10). Understanding this, we can see the folly in Lucifer's original bet against the certainty of God.

You may be saying, "this article makes me feel uneasy". I feel as though my life is already spent, that I am an embarrassment to myself, my family, and my friends". Maybe you've lost it all – lost your home, your spouse, your children. All of the good advice you've received along the way to change has been lost as you went your own way. What now? Can God even forgive me?

Your sins and regrets may seem overwhelming and great. Know this – God is greater. The only thing that stands between you and God is…you. Your pride. Your doubt. Your gamble on your own divinity. The devil whispers in your ear and says, "Follow me. I know the way". The devil is a liar. He is the father of all lies. Don't let him bind you up so that you are eternally separated from God. Break loose of your pride and regrets. Turn your mind and heart to God. God is waiting for you, just as the father of the prodigal son waited for him.

Beloved, God's love for you knows no bounds. The Psalmist says, "Oh taste and see that the Lord is good…," (Psalm 34:8). He is good. And He forgives. And He will forgive you, if you but ask. You are not a mistake. You have been endowed with great potential – potential that can only be fulfilled by discovering God's path for you. Your life is His most precious gift. Don't waste it. It's never too late to say, "God, I am sorry for what I have done, and for those I've hurt. Please forgive me, I repent of my sins against you". When you do, the days of gambling your life away will be over and you will be re-born with His purpose in your heart.

Be blessed!

I AM MY FATHER'S CHILD

Upon reflecting on this assertive statement, what stands out underscores the level of responsibility a father has for His child. But wait a minute; doesn't the child also have some responsibility? Indeed! Let's consider first, the father's role with respect to provision, security and in direct proportion to his relationship to God.

The father sees to it that the welfare of the child is well intact. The welfare in view encompasses, but is not limited to such things as shelter, clothing, and sustenance. The father fosters an environment relative to God's prescription of child rearing until the child is of adult age. One key aspect in being successful at child rearing lies in the understanding of your child; bear in mind that children differ characteristically. There should be no occasion for comparing one child to another. This is a common error most parents commit, i.e., comparing one's child to that of the neighbor's across the street or even to any of their sibling(s). This is one sure way of having your respect murdered by your child. Don't do it!

Understanding the distinction between physical and spiritual realms is paramount. Since their functions derive from different dimensions, nurturing the two constitutes tasks of magnitude consequence. Physical nurturing happens naturally. Spiritual, on the other hand does not. Spiritual nurturing requires painstaking, purposeful undertaking. It cannot be left to chances, it must be modeled. For instance, a child may have no difficulty going to the refrigerator looking for something to eat, but it is highly unlikely that the same child will open the Word of God looking for spiritual food to eat.

The task of rearing a child is such that a lackadaisical, incensed person should not get involved in. Inculcating his choice values, it is the father's responsibility to nurture and chastise negative behaviors with meekness when necessary. While being cautious that exasperating a child would initiate rebellion and inhibit learning, conversely love, grace, patience and longsuffering in the context of coaching should not be carried out devoid of reliance on the one who has given you that child.

Atmosphere in the home must be such that, "Where the Spirit of the Lord is, there is liberty". On the basis of Godly injunctions, the father provides core values. In other words, a family legacy deemed worthy of transcendence for posterity at large. In implementing his task, the father resists the temptation to adopt a democratic system that is out of character for a child to initiate how he/she should be raised.

Raising a child in the formative years before adulthood is purely monarchical in style, since the father is the authority figure in his child's life. While being resolute in his wherewithal, a conscientious father must with utmost necessity abhor autocratic (iron fist) leadership in his home. Unconscionably, an iron fist leadership will engender strife in the family. The father must consult wisdom (God's Wisdom) and courage when at a crossroad and has no idea where to turn. Solomon, Deuteronomy, Joshua, and Paul's admonition to Timothy should be companion books for the father raising a God fearing child.

Nevertheless, the child's adherence to the father's governance is tantamount to the child's world view of authority figures at large, what is more, the child's view of God. My child pay heed to my counsel and live.

Undoubtedly, children of this generation face enormous challenges, since they must stay current with what is in vogue. But what is in vogue may not necessarily be advantageous for most children's consumption. Herein is wisdom quintessential. The child needs parental guidance to assist in navigating through the changing worlds around them. The child must be made aware that family setups are different. What might be obtainable in X's family may be disastrous to attempt in Y's family, particularly if X and Y have differing world views. There is bound to be information collusion. The application of "different strokes for different folks" is quite apropos in this instance.

To avoid information collusion the child should be responsive to the father's wisdom. Having friends with whom the child exchanges ideas poses no danger, however, if the ideas conflict with the family values and structure, the child should seek the father's wisdom in all matters pertaining to their family orientation.

Now, there are those who might argue, I didn't have a father figure in my life, yet I turned out okay. What do you say about that? I thank God for your life. You turned out okay; it was not purely due to your intelligence, but to God's grace. I will dare to say, that at some point in your life you will have preferred differently, i.e., to have a father present in your life, assuming he is not a monstrous, abusive father. But we are not talking about that, rather we are talking of a father who cares for the wellbeing of his family.

The person who argues against a father figure in the family, truth be told, will agree with me that during your preadolescent to adolescent years, you will have sought counsel from someone who stood out as a father figure to you. Someone you looked up to. Perhaps a teacher or a coach of some sort. The fact that you considered seeking guidance for whatever reason from that teacher or that coach indicated that you sought an authority figure in your life; hence it confirms that a father figure is invaluable in the family. Undoubtedly, it must be said that not all fathers have the wherewithal to deal with tough situations. Be that as it may, a child thrives well when a loving father is around.

A child needs a father, a loving father, a God honoring father to coach the child through the maze of life. It is much, much easier for a child to deal with challenging situations knowing with confidence that they will have someone to "bounce" things off of instead of trying to figure things out alone. The father is there to encourage, support and provide loving arms when the child bleeds from rejection and bruises inflicted by the world outside the comfort of home. The child honors the father when the child takes the father's counsel and becomes successful. Then the child indeed has become a wise child and can truly say, I am my father's child.

—Rev. Christian Nwakaihe

ARE WE RUNNING ON EMPTY?

Consider the following facts:
- Average annual intake for Americans is:
  - Between 150 and 177 lbs of sugar
  - 51 lbs of French fries per person annually
  - 300 lbs of fruit per person (over 50% is in canned products with added sugar)
  - 92 lbs of tomatoes (80% is processed with sugar added)
  - 600 million Big Macs
  - 20 billion hotdogs
  - 8 billion chickens
- 1/3 of population is obese; 62% of adults are overweight
- Over 1 million cardiovascular deaths annually
- Over ½ million cancer deaths annually
- 8% have diabetes; nearly 6 million have diabetes and don't know it.

So based on what we are consuming we can see a correlation to diseases that people are dying from considering we now know saturated fats, sugars and simple carbs are related as has been discussed throughout the media.

Looking at USRDA for guidance is not the answer to the health issues facing the broad population at large because the RDA (Recommendation Daily Allowances) are based on minimum requirements to, in my words, sustain life under optimum conditions. For example those recommendations don't address: the level of nutrients that are being wasted by the drugs we take (i.e., statin/cholesterol and other drugs, and over the counter meds such as aspirin, etc.), the degenerative illnesses prevalent in our society (i.e., high blood pressure, diabetes, etc.), the environmental poisons we ingest daily or the nutrient deficient produce on the market today.

Another example is, the USRDA's recommendation for Thiamine is 1.2 mg (enough to prevent beriberi); there are sugar coated cereals that will provide a significant % of that amount in one serving, however if your goal is to be vibrantly healthy with regards to today's demands you may need numerous times that amount to get to your desired benefit. According to Alex Duarte (PhD-nutritionist) high Thiamine doses have been linked to a healthy nervous system and improved brain function (it's been used for epileptic patient's neuropsychological functions), low doses (by some standards USRDA levels) have been linked to depression, heart disease, neurological disorders, and even canker sores. There is a clear possible benefit of taking additional Thiamin; however no proven risk of detriment.

As a society, and on a smaller scale as a community, we must be more aware, diligent and proactive about maintaining our health. There are 6 physical fundamental keys to health: Oxygen, Water, Nutrient, Digestion/Elimination, Exercise, and Rest. Each one is a topic of discussion in itself.

6 Keys to good Health: Oxygen, Water, Nutrition, Digestion/Elimination, Exercise, and Rest.

Digestion-Do we understand how our body really metabolizes the nutrients we take in?

Did You Know?
- By age 50 many people will produce only 15% of the hydrochloric acid they produced at age 25.

- Americans spent $107 billion on drugs and antacids to fight digestive ailments in 1992.
- 60-70 million Americans suffer from digestive disease.
- Digestive problems cost Americans $50 billion each year in medical bills and absence from work.

 The divine unit that it is, digestion starts before we even touch a piece of food. From the moment we think of the food we are to ingest the body begins preparation for the digestive process. The thought of food signals nerve impulses to the gastrointestinal tract. These signals put the digestive system on alert; our mouth begins to water, the stomach starts to contract in preparation to receive the food. The pancreas, a glandular organ that releases enzymes essential to digestion, starts to secrete chemicals that will break down the food.

 Inside the mouth the food is ground and broken down by the teeth while the saliva moistens, lubricates, and begins to digest the starch from the food into smaller molecules. Most <u>(60+ %) of the **starches** we consume are digested in the mouth.</u> A chemical reaction occurs that takes the starches (Hydrogen, Oxygen, Carbon components) and produces water to moisten and assist the peristaltic action to push the food down the esophagus into the stomach. The food will start the 2nd digestive process here at the "pre-digestive stomach" where the enzymes from the mouth mix with the enzymes from the food and churn for about an hour. Due to the lack of enzymes in our food not much is going on here for most people. After that time the stomach begins to pull minerals (sodium, hydrogen, chloride) from the bloodstream to create hydrochloric acid (HCI). Parasites are killed here due to the high acidic value (pH of 3.5) now in the stomach. Pepsin (an enzyme) is created to break down protein and create amino acids. Minerals are derived from the food and broken down to a size that can be used in the small intestine.

If the pH (acid/alkaline) level doesn't drop to 3 (on a scale of 2-9) we get rotting of the food and it sends acid gas up the esophagus and we get acid reflux or GERD (gastro esophagus reflex disorder). Acid reflux can be due to lack of hydrochloric acid or lack of mucus lining the stomach.

The next step in the digestive process is at the Duodenum (entrance to the small intestines); at this point the hypothalamus (which is constantly monitoring the functions) sends a signal to the gallbladder to send bile (very alkaline) to the intestines through the common bile duct to degrease the fats. The pancreas then sends amylase, lipase, and protease (3 types of enzymes) to further break down the food. Then through 26 ft. of intestine, absorption takes place to nourish our various body systems, glands, and vital organs.

DIGESTION TIPS:
1. Chew your food thoroughly-digestion begins in the mouth.
2. Avoid liquids while eating-they dilute the digestive fluids.
3. Avoid eating under stress-your body won't optimally provide energy to nervous and digestive systems simultaneously.

TAKE AWAY: Throughout the above brief on digestion you saw the term Enzyme. By now you know the importance of enzymes as an integral part of the digestive process; however you may not have a very good appreciation of what they are or how we can insure we are getting the most from them.

Enzymes are protein molecules that are essential to life because they (digestive enzymes) serve to break the food we ingest down to a form where our bodies can absorb it and assimilate it to be used for nutrition and energy; in addition metabolic enzymes serve as catalysts and regulators for the tens of thousands of functions our bodies perform daily including: breathing, smelling, tasting, defending our bodies against disease, and even thinking, to name a few. Some medical researchers believe there is a correlation between enzyme deficiency and illness/disease such as Cancer, Arthritis, aging, skin disease, allergies, obesity, and heart disease.

We are all born with enzymes and as we age our supply begins to diminish. In fact an average new born has 100 times more enzymes than a typical 70 year old, and by the time we are 20 we only have about 2 times the enzymes of a 70 year old. Although our personal store of enzymes is limited, enzymes are available in raw foods and also available in supplement form. The problem with getting our enzymes from raw food is most of us don't/can't ingest enough raw food to compensate for the cooked and processed food we eat that depletes our store of digestive enzymes.

Early signs of possible enzyme deficiency are: allergies, belching, gas, bloating, fatigue, nutritional deficiencies, headaches, constipation, diarrhea, heartburn and yeast infections. These signs are so prevalent some people consider them normal; however they are anything but normal and could be a reflection that the body cannot process the food that is eaten. Eating enzyme deficient food compromises the digestive process in all its stages: digestion, absorption, assimilation, and elimination.

So what's the solution? Eat more raw fruits and vegetables and take a natural enzyme supplement from a highly quality source.

WHEN NOTHING IS ENOUGH

Dear Readers,

While everything is up in a row with the economy, we thought about our mother's cooking. Back then in the "good old days" we didn't have a large choice of condiments or spices around the house but her cooking was the best! Spices are more readily and reasonably priced today so you will be blessed to get as many kinds of spices as you want for soups, main dishes and all kinds of meats.

As I was shopping the other day, I bought a ham. It reminded me of the split pea soup that my mother used to make. After most of the meat was gone, she would take the ham bone and put it in a stock pot with water and add a package of split peas and an onion and if we were really lucky she had a carrot or two that was left in the icebox. She would slice them and add them to the soup along with a pinch of salt and pepper. Following the directions on the package, mother would simmer those peas on low heat until a smooth delicious meal was ready to warm your soul.

Have you ever heard of pig's feet with lima beans? How about succotash with sliced hotdogs mixed together? There are so many different low cost meals that can carry you through rough patches. Every culture, community and families from all over the world has their own memories of these "make-do meals". Below are a few tips and tidbits we shared at a meeting one evening.

DON'T ASK, DON'T TELL MEAL HELPERS.
World's best filler – **water**
World's best filler for meat - **bread**
World's greatest camouflage - **gravy**
When everything else fails- **eat peanut butter**

LESS IS MORE RECIPES:

<u>WING – A – DING DING</u>
Take 9 chicken wings, fry, cut all three joints & stack in a pyramid.
Looks like a mountain of chicken – Presentation is everything!

<u>POOR MAN'S DOUGHNUTS</u>
Take canned biscuits & cut hole in middle using the top of the vinegar bottle
Heat approximately ¾ cup of vegetable oil.
Fry both donuts and holes until golden brown
Drain on paper towel
Mix cinnamon and sugar in a bowl. Pour some of the mixture in a brown paper bag, drop the warm donuts in the bag and shake until the doughnuts are covered and you've lost enough calories to eat them. Kids love to help!

<u>NO FLOUR PEANUT BUTTER COOKIES</u>
1 cup sugar
1 egg
1 cup creamy peanut butter
½ tsp. vanilla
Mix well
Drop on cookie sheet
Heat oven 300-325 degrees, Bake: 13 minutes
Let cool and add fruit on top: cherries strawberries, etc.

Thank God for these recipes and tips. The Bible tells us to be content with what we have and that the Lord's grace is sufficient for us. He will always provide for His people. Oh yeah, by the way, remember: Don't pass by a penny on the ground-Pennies make dollars! Dollars make millions!

SWEET MULTI~PEPPER TOMATO SAUCE

Ingredients:

1 pkg. of whole wheat or whole grain pasta
1 large jar of your favorite spaghetti sauce (add more if you would like it saucier)
1 large sweet onion
1 medium onion
1 teaspoon chopped garlic
2 large green bell peppers
1 orange pepper
1 red pepper
1 yellow pepper
2 packages sliced portabella mushrooms (cut into cubes)
1 teaspoon basil
1 teaspoon oregano
1 bay leaf
1 large carrot (optional)
3 tablespoons extra virgin olive oil

1. Boil whole grain or whole wheat pasta (follow pkg. instructions to prepare)
2. Thinly slice onion and peppers.
3. Cut portabella mushrooms into small cubes

4. In sauce pan- sauté mushrooms in 1 tablespoon of extra virgin olive oil until mushrooms make juice-(set aside).
5. In large pot add remaining olive oil. Sautee onions.
6. Add garlic and green, orange, and red peppers -Mix well and cook until peppers become tender. Add mushrooms.
7. Add spaghetti sauce and mix ingredients well.
8. Add oregano, basil and bay leaf. Mix well.

Let ingredients simmer for at least 30 minutes, stir occasionally.

Note: If sauce is too tart (cut a carrot in half and add to sauce to sweeten).

Top off dish with a sprinkle of parmesan cheese.

—Joyce Hancock-Williams

IT'S GOING TO RAIN: A FAMILY REUNION

Planning and preparing for the Daniels' first family reunion was hard work. It took a great deal of time and lots of energy. Some family members were focused on looking for a place, deciding the menu and choosing the music and entertainment. Others were making travel plans (some from long distances) to join the rest of the family. The Daniel's family was coming together from many different directions to unite as one unit but there is always that family "thing" that Satan tries to use to divide the family and cause chaos. God's word is full of warning labels that alert us to certain things which are harmful to our spiritual health. In Proverbs 6:16-19 it states: There are six things which the LORD hates, yes, seven which are an abomination to Him: haughty eyes, a lying tongue, and hands that shed innocent blood, a heart that devises wicked plans, feet that run rapidly to evil, a false witness who utters lies, and one who spreads strife among brothers. A mind that thinks of doing things will produce a spirit that makes one over estimate himself and under estimate others.

In the midst of all the goings on it is important not to lose sight of the reason we get together. Reunions are a time for meeting family members to get to know them better. A time to reminisce about those who have passed, those who have been born, who got married and the "good old days". Reunions can be good bonding events.

It was a beautiful Saturday afternoon without a rain cloud in the sky. The families began to gather together under the tent that was pitched out in the open yard. There was plenty of food and activities were under way. The children were playing in the lawn sprinklers to cool off from the heat of the day. You see, God is a generous God and the Bible says "they drink their fill of the abundance of your house; and you give them to drink of the river of your delight." Finally everyone joined in with some of the activities, but then all of a sudden it began to sprinkle drops of rain. Everyone continued doing whatever pleased them. A few minutes later, it started raining harder. The family began gathering under the tent into small groups. Although this was a "reunion" designed to have everyone get together to have fun, be filled with happiness and get to know one another, the people collected into their own little groups.

Soon the winds got stronger and blew harder and a few of the people looked as if they had been drawn closer together but not close enough. The winds got even stronger and the rain came pouring down. It got very crowded under that tent. Some people had to stand outside of the tent in the rain. The family had no other choice but to get closer. There were people standing in puddles of water forcing them to move even closer together under the tent. They had gotten so close that there was no room to move. This situation caused everyone to start talking to one another and it didn't matter whether you knew the person standing next to you or not. The next thing you know, the wind started blowing so hard that the tent blew away like a kite in the sky.

Ephesians 5:15-17 says: Be very careful, then, how you live - not as unwise but as wise, making the most of every opportunity, because the days are evil. Therefore do not be foolish, but understand what the Lord's will is. Since none of us know our "Use by Date", better known as our "Expiration Date" we must capture the opportunity to brighten our world with the love of Christ today. We should do everything in our power to live each day as if it is our last.

—Rocky Evans

HE WAS THERE ALL THE TIME!

THIS IS A STORY I DIDN'T WANT TO TELL…a story that I've kept hidden deep within my heart for many years. My childhood was filled with memories of rejection, hurt and pain while growing up in a home with an abusive father. But it's not only my story. It's for all the women who have experienced any type of abuse. It is difficult to have a healthy relationship with the opposite sex, if you don't seek God for answers, and get counseling to break the pattern of abuse. As I reflect back on my life, I know that God was with me all the time. I had to acknowledge that I had a problem.

Unfortunately, I did not seek counseling for my problem, nor did I know how much God loved me at the time. I went through two failed marriages before realizing that I had been looking for love in all the wrong places. I married each of my husbands for the wrong reason. I knew later on in my life that I needed to love myself first before finding a man to love me. But I did not know what true love was and had no idea where to search for answers. I later found this chapter in the Bible that gave me a clear analysis of the true meaning of love. Now I know.

I recommend that everyone consider reading (I Corinthians 1-13) to understand the real meaning of love. If I had known the key elements of love, I would have known if someone loved and cared about me for the right reasons. Without genuine love and commitment to each other, a marriage will not endure the storms.

My recommendation is that you take time to get to know your mate. Observe them carefully during the dating stage. Look closely at the way they treat you during this time. Find out what their likes and dislikes are. Don't make the same mistakes as I did. Recognize the difference between lust and love. If someone loves you for your body only, and the relationship is based only on lust, the relationship will not endure the storms in a marriage. I realized too late in my marriage that our marriage was in trouble. Once the fights started they quickly went from verbal to physical abuse. It seemed to happen so quickly. My feelings of love for my husband was gone, it had really turned into hatred. By the time the marriage ended, my heart had been broken into so many pieces. I still had some hope that I could make it work; just maybe I could make him love me. I tried so hard to be a good homemaker. Our home was always kept neat and clean, and I took good care of my children. But there is one thing I would like to share with women; nothing will make a man love you if he did not feel love for you from the start of the relationship. My husband's only interest was the sex. It was all about lust.

After we married, we lived with his parents for two years. We probably would have stayed there a lot longer because my husband was satisfied living there with them. We continued to stay with his parents until I became pregnant with my second son. I remember walking with my child, looking for an apartment every day. I finally found an apartment in a government housing complex. The rent was only fifty dollars a month. This happened a long time of ago when renting apartments didn't cost a lot. I felt so happy that I had finally found a place of my own, a place to start over with my family. I also thought this would be an opportunity to save money and then be able to buy our own home. I began to take in sewing for people; making dresses, coats and gowns, etc. to help supplement our income. I designed clothes for fashion shows, dances, and gowns for special parties.

I had to work through the nights to complete many of these outfits. It was overwhelming during the holiday seasons; especially Christmas and Easter. The verbal and physical abuse increased between my husband and me. It was then that I realized my marriage was disintegrating. Deeply hurt and disillusioned about all the things happening in marriage, I didn't know where to turn. My life at this point was being torn apart, my husband even threatened to leave me. I made every attempt to try and save my marriage. At first, I tried to communicate with my husband. I was hoping at least; he would try and understand my feelings. I realized at this point that my husband only cared about sex, love did not exist.

For the sake of the children, I stayed in a bad relationship. I wanted desperately for this marriage to work. It was a difficult period in my life, but in retrospect, I can still see God's plan in what was happening in my life.

We purchased a very lovely home in a beautiful neighborhood with good schools and wonderful neighbors. I was still hoping my marriage would work. God blessed us financially with a refund from the housing complex for being model citizens and keeping our apartment immaculate. God blesses us in miraculous ways.

Before we moved into our new home, I was able to get a job away from home. The extra income was needed to help with household expenses. My husband never wanted me to work outside of the home, but his salary was not enough to support the family. The money from my new job helped to pay the closing cost on our home. Once I started to earn a pay check, my husband then wanted to use the money for other things. I couldn't understand what he was thinking. At first, he didn't want me to work and now he wants to take the money I'm making and use it for something other than our bills. He was in charge of paying the monthly bills. I know now that I made a mistake by not taking the time to share in the responsibility of paying the bills. I would have known the bills were not getting paid on time or not at all.

When it finally came time to move out of the apartment, and into our new home; to my surprise my husband was very happy that we were moving. He couldn't wait to move into our new place. He moved the dressers without even taking the clothes out of the drawers. We settled in gradually and things were looking good for us.

My mother was an angel. She was part of the plan God had for my life. She took care of my children and helped out with everything to help make our lives as easy as possible. I was so grateful for what she was doing. She was there physically, and spiritually praying for me all the time. I know today my mother was the reason that God came into my life later on and is still present in my life today.

I met a co-worker, who became my best girlfriend. She knew how to design clothes. She had a beautiful figure and was the perfect model. She could wear all types of clothing and look great. We became a team. She designed and I sewed the outfits for her. I began making clothes for her to wear when she attended special events with her husband. Everyone who saw her outfits wanted to know where she got them. She loved to dress elegantly and wear the latest fashions; and her designs were incredible. Our designs began to expand in many areas; such as fashion shows with models and organizational fund raising. The extra money was a great help.

Hanging with his friends, my husband couldn't and didn't keep a job. It was always someone else's fault. I no longer had the same feelings for my husband that I had when we first met. I became exhausted trying to make our marriage work. I had given it my all and nothing worked. As I look back, I started doing things that I was not proud of like drinking and smoking with my girlfriends. That behavior didn't solve my problems. Later, I discovered that my husband had stopped paying the bills. Our final fight as husband and wife came one night after a dance. Unbeknownst to me, his girlfriend was also at this dance. My husband wanted to take me home so he could return to the dance and spend time with his girlfriend. On the way home, an argument ensued, in which my husband severely battered my eyes and my head.

We separated. I found an apartment for my children and me. Even though I was heartbroken over our separation, my work was a comfort. After being alone for awhile, I met someone; he asked me out on a date and I accepted. Somehow my husband found out about it (to this day I don't know how). He found a way to get into my car and tamper with the brakes. He followed us on the road and tried to kill us. Thank God we were alright, but my car was totaled. I could not understand my husband's behavior at all; he didn't want to be with me, yet he tried to kill me because someone took an interest in me. My husband had already remarried. The relationship with this man did not last.

Time passed and I began to feel alone. Even with my children, my life felt empty. My girlfriend knew a minister who felt the same way. He was looking for a wife. She never shared the reason why the minister wanted a wife. I had been through so much; I was not looking for another husband at this time. I needed to do some soul searching of myself before I entered into another relationship.

Eventually I accepted an invitation from the minister to go out on a date. We dated for one year. During this time, the minister treated me kindly. I found myself being drawn to him because of his kindness. We eventually got married. After marrying him, I found out why he was looking for someone. He only wanted a woman who was hard working, to clean and cook for him and to fill the void of loneliness in his life. The marriage didn't last long, it was annulled. It was never consummated in the first place.

My searching led me to a closer encounter with God. My prayers went up to God from home to work that He would fill me with his Holy Spirit. I could not live my life without Him anymore. This is still true for me today. A life without God is no life at all, God does answer prayers.

A transformation took place in my life while I was on vacation. While washing dishes, the spirit spoke to me and said "go and pray." I immediately stopped washing dishes and went into my bedroom, fell down on my knees and began to pray. I spoke openly to God. I said to him, I don't want to live like this anymore. If you don't come into my heart and fill me with your Holy Spirit and love right now, I don't want to live anymore. "At this time, I was not thinking about my children or anything else, except that I had lost my will to go on. At that very moment I was filled with so much love that I thought it would choke me. I tried to see the spirit that had entered my bedroom, but I could only see a white mist leaving the room. It was a small mist, but carried a very powerful lilac smell that was so sweet. It was the Holy Spirit. As God's Holy Spirit began to engulf me, I cried and cried uncontrollably, repenting for my sins. After my encounter with the Holy Spirit, I knew that God had changed my life.

Returning back to finish the dishes, everything was crystal clear to me. Looking out the kitchen window, God had opened my heart and given me discernment about people. My life had truly changed and I would never be the same.

I was overjoyed that God had found me, I was only a small grain of sand, a pebble on the beach and he had chosen me out of the world to be his own. He planted his Word in my mind and heart. He revealed to me the love that I had been searching for all my life. Through the Word of God, my purpose in life had been revealed.

My advice to all those who are going through problems is hold on, be strong and pray. God answers our prayers. He controls everything and He knows everything. Nothing is too hard for God, He will never disappoint you. For those of you that do not know God as your personal savior, whether you are in church or not, truly get to know him. Embrace the love that God has for you.

You are special to Him, He sent His only begotten Son to die for our sins and to give us eternal life. I will never get over how much He loves me. He loves you the same way. He says, "come as you are". You don't have to change anything to come to Him. God will do the work in you to make you who He wants you to be. My marriages didn't last, but God will. He says, "I will never leave you nor forsake you". Through all of this, God saw fit to keep me. He kept me and saved me by His grace through faith. There is one thing that I am sure of, GOD IS REAL, He was there all the time!

GROW YOUR OWN OPRAH

She's smart! She's sassy, loving and she brings to the world and to the workplace a bounty of riches. She makes us think, she's positive and spiritual. What a lady! "That's Oprah." She opens our eyes, hearts and minds to challenge the unknown. She wants us to seek out the most positive ways of living in a world where the odds are extremely hard to achieve. She makes us yearn for the deep knowledge within each of us as we travel life's journey. Oprah is a self-made woman. She shares that with us daily in her walk of life. Who's this brassy lady? What makes her strive to perfection? "That's Oprah."

From the time of her birth in Mississippi, deep in the south, the rise to power, wealth, fame and grace came at a very high price. A big, powerful, beautiful soul, that shares herself in such a way that it forces us to grow the Oprah inside of us. Those that have negative thoughts, ideas about what they can achieve, need to stop and listen to this great lady. We need to take what she gives in her words and deeds to each other and see the positive side of life. "That's Oprah." We know that sometimes it gets hard, but Oprah brings life to us all. She nurtures and inspires each of us to seek within for our own greatness.

Oprah is a shining example to so many people around the world. She encourages us to embrace our gifts and talents and makes our dreams a reality. Seeing her life unfold from start until the present helps us to believe that there's hope for us. She helps us tap into that spiritual core that we all so desperately need. She's a beacon of light that no matter what walk of life we come from or what we have gone through, she encourages us all to be the best that we can be. She uses her love, money and success to show that no matter what others think we are incapable of doing, we can overcome. Oprah wants us to be more loving toward our families, co-workers, people in our communities, and all those that we meet along the way.

The greatest gifts we can give our children and family members is to encourage them, be positive role models, and help our children as well as ourselves to achieve our goals. We can do this through our actions and positive words of encouragement. As we encourage others to preserve and overcome, that's the Oprah in our own lives. When we build a victorious foundation within ourselves, we can share that joy and excitement with others, along the way.

Let's not share our pain and guilt on other individuals. Let's not criticize, hurt and try to kill the spirit in one another. Let's come together and work on one accord, and let our lights shine daily. We are the children that God created in His own image. Let us help others to reach and achieve all their dreams while we are on this earth. Let's not have our pride stand in the way of loving and caring for each other. At least that's what Oprah tells us!

When I reflect back on my own life and the various situations I encountered along the way, I understand more clearly now that Oprah has taught me a lot about being wise in relationships and friendship along the way. It is hard for us to receive and give compliments to others. Whether it is our outfits, or our body beauty, we easily choose the road, "It's all about me". Each of us has a unique sphere of influence, and that influence can be used for evil or for good. We all should use our influence for good, just like, what's her name? "Oprah." Instead we have those individuals that have positive and negative effects toward each other in their relationship as friend. Janet is a positive person and Bonnie is a negative person. Roberta is a negative person and Lois is a positive person. Other people I have met along my path in life care more about prestige and what can be done for them, rather than being kind to others they meet.

Why do we try so hard to hurt one another? God made us to be loving and encouraging toward each other. But it becomes so easy to feel less important than others when we think that they have more talents than we do. That's not what Oprah wants us to do. When we as a people can learn to be supportive to each other and recognize all our various gifts and talents than we can learn to help each other reach their full potentials in life. When we help each other to express their greatness, we embrace the Oprah in all our lives.

Growing our Oprah simply means helping and supporting each other along the way. Recognize and help each other to reach their potential, giving them the opportunity to express their greatness. A slight twist on the golden rule applies here: "NURTURE THE OPRAH IN SOMEONE ELSE AND SOMEONE WILL NURTURE THE OPRAH IN YOU!" I know that God works for us by working through us. The more we give the more we have to give. It's not only our material gifts, that's returned to us, it's the love and support we give to others also. It's returned in far greater measure than given, when we freely give. When we nurture the greatness in others, we fertilize the good in them, helping them to focus their attention on those things that are worthwhile and positive. Encourage another and watch them and yourself flourish. When we elevate one, we elevate the whole. "That's what Oprah has been telling the world."

There's always something special we can honor in others, something that deserves and need acknowledgement. The world can be cruel and crushing! Anyone doing anything positive needs to be and should be encouraged. Everyone can use some positive reinforcements or feedback. We all do better with a pat on the back, "job well done, keep up the good work."

The world is not set up for everyone to be rich, famous and deemed worthwhile in the public arena. However, there are Oprah's in the making that will be spiritually powerful and great credits to their communities. We all can help an Oprah we know to grow! Recognize, acknowledge, encourage and honor the God in them. Proclaim their greatness enthusiastically to them and to the world. After all, there's a little Oprah seed in all of us, pleading. "WHAT ABOUT ME!" All it need is a little love, compassion, recognition, encouragement, and the words YOU CAN.

CHICKEN AND RICE

2 cups rice
4 cups of water
1/8 stick of butter or margarine
1 stem of scallion

Cut up chicken and remove skin and fat. Season the chicken with adobe seasoning, black pepper, thyme, and scallions. Place chicken in covered container and allow it to soak overnight in refrigerator. The next day, remove chicken from refrigerator and put in a Dutch pot with 4 cups of water and rice. Simmer until well done.

—Rev. Claudette Washington

THOUGHTS ON HARD TIMES

I can remember moving to Brooklyn NY when I was four years old, although originally my parents came from very hard working families in New Jersey. It was there in New York that my father got a job as a mechanic for the Brooklyn Police Department and mother found employment in a factory. She worked in that factory until she became ill and couldn't work any more. That's when our hard times began.

Our main source of family income now was provided by my father. During this time for whatever reason, he started hanging out with the wrong crowd of people. He began drinking alcohol. After awhile it seemed to have taken over his life. He continued to hang around these people. They had such a negative effect on him that he began to shirk his responsibilities when it came to caring for his family. Back then it was only my sister Marion and me that he had to care for. We were always hungry and needing something. One day we were so hungry we started shaking. We had a very caring mother. She would give us what little food we had and she wouldn't eat. She would just tell us that she wasn't hungry.

We knew father had money because he worked but he wouldn't give mother any for food or rent. If she hadn't looked in his pockets for money when he was asleep we wouldn't have had anything at all. What she did find provided very little help. During those days if your rent wasn't paid you would literally be put out on the street. I mean all of your furniture, clothing and even your children would be placed on the sidewalk!

My sister Theresa came next. When she was born our maternal grandfather came to New York to bring us to New Jersey to live with him. Everything was going well until father came to New Jersey begging our mother to come back to New York. My mother went back to him which caused us to be without all over again. You see, my mother loved my father very much and she was taught to love and to be a good wife to him. Dad's same old habits started all over again and eventually there was no more food but there was plenty of those two fighting. Grandfather wanted dad to leave us alone but every time he intervened, mother would take sides with dad.

Daddy used to beat mother. He would go to jail and when he got out she would take him back. In those days there was no welfare but there were relief programs that we couldn't apply for until dad went to jail for beating my mother. When he got out of jail she would take him back, get pregnant and the whole cycle would start all over again. Our family just grew larger and larger. Every time my father came home from jail, my mother would have another baby. He just loved hanging in the streets with his friends, getting drunk and beating mother. Mommy and daddy had a total of seventeen children in all but only ten of us survived. This may seem strange, but our happiest days were when daddy went to jail!

My grandfather's farm didn't have running water so we had to pump water from the well and carry it back in order to cook and clean and do everything that water was needed for. This was the only way we were able to get water. There were no street lights in the county in those days so if we didn't get the water during the day, we would have to go and pump it in the dark of night. We also cut wood for cooking and heating the house. Our shoes wore out so badly that they would fall apart, but we managed by wearing someone else's hand me downs. Whatever someone would give us would be used. Whenever my mother was able to work she would do housework for people. The people she worked for loved her so much that they would help her sometimes. Our clothes were handmade and I made my clothes from flower bags and whatever fabric material I could get my hands on. We had very cold winters and used wood burning or coal burning stoves to keep us warm. Whenever we had a shortage of blankets we would use our coats as well.

Sometimes some of the store keepers would give my grandfather a half case of chicken for us to cook. If we got a chicken, it went into the stew pot with anything else in the refrigerator. We never fried it because it had to stretch. We used the cabbage leaves that people threw away as a meal which would be cooked in fatback. Sometimes we'd have fried cornmeal cake or flour cakes and put jelly on them. I remember my mother making a meal consisting of a few beans, an onion, a small piece of meat for seasoning along with tomatoes and celery. We had no idea that beans were a good source of fiber. We were thankful that we had a meal to eat! When grand pop came over with the garbage truck, we would jump on the truck to check for fruit. We would take an apple or an orange that may have had a bad spot or bad side on it, cut away the rotten part and eat the rest of it. Nothing and I mean nothing was wasted!

I remember we lived in a house about two houses away from my mother's brother and his family. My uncle was a fine man and a good father. They had running water and a bathroom in the house. Every day they had a table full of food! They had large dinners every night. He had eleven children and they all wore "good" clothes and shoes. They even had a television in the house. On Christmas, everyone in their family received one large "good" present. Our hearts ached because we had nothing. My mother came from a very fine family. They wanted for nothing.

Our hearts ached because we had nothing. I will never forget the fact that we never had a Thanksgiving Dinner and how for Christmas, we had a tree that we got from the woods. We would dress the tree with paper things as ornaments. Growing up we didn't have television until we were teenagers. We did have a radio and enjoyed listening to the stories and news programs. In those days we didn't run the streets. Baseball and kick-ball were our pastimes and some of the boys would make go carts for toys.

Eventually I grew up, got married and had two sons. The marriage didn't work so I had to raise my children alone. They didn't have designer clothes but I gave them food, shelter and love. This was my first priority. After my marriage ended, I worked for thirty-two years at Johnson and Johnson to maintain my home and take care of my children. We were never homeless. When Christ came into my life I was alone but not lonely and I no longer had to look for love. You see, Jesus fulfills my every need and comfort. I must say to everyone, please keep a positive attitude about yourself. This is the key to success in life. When your nose is up in the air, you only get bad smells and this will get you nowhere.

Hard times come to us for a reason. One is to change us into better people. Discouragement based on how life has not worked out the way we thought it should will always come. Sometimes people will feel like they want to kill themselves because they don't want to bear the pressures that life will present to them. During this difficult time in my life I thought about ending it all. Then I looked at my children and thought to myself, I may have had it hard but I must work hard to raise my sons who didn't ask to come into this world. I was determined that I did not want my sons to go through what I went through as a child. I used my experience to better their lives.

My old dreams are gone but God gave me a better dream. I wanted to be a designer. I ended up with models, having great fashion shows and had wonderful designs. If I had ended my life I would have missed out on a wonderful life and family. I now have four of the most beautiful grandchildren and one of the loveliest daughter-in-laws ever! I also have an extended family of sons and daughters.

There is more, so much more that I could tell you but for those of you who are reading this, I would like to say to you that you can make it. God gave me this life and I refuse to let anyone or anything in this life bring me to a point of wanting to end it. So sit down and take a few minutes to get yourself together and realize that life is a blessing. Trust God, hold on and He will see you through.

—SALLIE PROCTOR

YOUTH PRAYER

To the Joshua Generation,

In this life we are faced with many options, some that will cause us to look different and some that will make us blend in. We have been given such a grace from God to stand out amongst the crowd and not just blend in. In a world that categorizes and labels you by your race, neighborhood, and financial status, we fight not to get caught up in the system.

As a son of Plainfield, NJ, I longed not to be just another statistic. I pressed and pushed hard so as not to end up into the system. It was not my desire to be different and stand out nor was it my doing. It was the hand of God upon me, leading me and guiding me to be who Christ designed me to be. I say this to say, you can do it too! Stand up to the systems of this world, the media and entertainment and the neighborhoods that want to draft you in. Stand up to the world and all of its double standards and make a difference with your life. In all realness the world can put on a great party that may look very entertaining and will almost draw us in but the reality is… the music will stop, the dancing will end and everyone has to eventually go back home. What will we return to? A place of peace or a place of chaos? That choice is yours. Making choices daily is what will determine the world we live in and how we live. I ask you Joshua Generation, the next and rising world, to make choices that will bring about great change, great hope and great victory.

THE ROSE OF SHARON COMMUNITY CHURCH

My high school principal used to say every morning during the announcements, "make it a great day, the choice is yours." So I say **make it a great life and world, the choice is yours!** Grace and peace!

A Simple Prayer for our Youth: Father, we may not know all the answers, we may not have all the pieces to the puzzle, but one thing we know is that you have it all figured out for each and every young and older person. Help us today to unlock the divine design and purpose you have for us. Protect us from all spirits of wrath and destruction that try to make us forget our identity. Help us not to hurt ourselves or others. Help us to remember we are royalty and we are princes and princesses. Father help us to love you, our family, our friends and our enemies. Teach us to walk in purity and holiness. Teach us to be like Christ at all times. Help us to cultivate an atmosphere where people can experience your love through us. Help us to remember to connect and fellowship with everyone no matter their background. Teach us to be a generation that will impact our communities and world with your message of love and grace. Father I ask you to cover our generation with the blood of Jesus. We decree and declare safety to every boy and girl, we decree and declare a good debt-free education for every young person. We decree and declare your divine blessings and love upon their lives. For we are the Next Generation! In Jesus' Name I pray, Amen!

REV. KYSHON S. MITCHELL
YOUTH PASTOR
ROSE OF SHARON COMMUNITY CHURCH,
PLAINFIELD, NJ

TROUBLES AND STORMS

We are at a point where we see (unless you are blind) blindness of the mind. Baby's are being born to our lovely young men and women, some out of wedlock. These young children are having so many children that one person was named "Octo" mom. They are also having children by different moms and dads. This is not love. It could be lust. And you could be ruining your future. Love does not mean "Legs Open Very Easily". You've hurt and stopped yourself from being successful in life. All of your dreams are placed on hold which you have no time for. Life moves on toward death. This is truth. Tomorrow doesn't belong to us, it's not ours or your children's. Don't get me wrong, having children is a blessing, the right way. Children look forward to a good life the same way you do. If you can't afford them on your own without government help, please don't bring this on these blessed little children.

Be a star in your own life's play. Hope and dream for a better life. It's yours to have as well as your children's. Try something that's a winner. You can bet on this, go to a quiet place by yourself. Your bedroom, basement, car or a special place where you won't be disturbed. Ask God for a one on one talk. He wants to hear from you. Believe it or not, He's waiting on you. Then, surrender your heart to Him. Once you've done that, you will want Him to lead you and guide you in everything you do. The Holy Spirit will be with you.

I can tell you that going to church will not make you rich in worldly ways and when you get there you will find people who are just like you. They were in the world but now they are looking for hope and how to please God. Looking with hope to God for eternal life and salvation. Hope is not in man but if you follow God your thoughts and ways of life will change so much for the better. It takes giving all that's within you to God to let him lead you everyday.

Just "think, think", you're at what age now? You were doing things your way up until now. Be it partying every weekend, drugging, sexing, gambling or just staying in your own home not thinking about God or anything. Sin was there just swimming around you trying to drown you. That's what Satan does, he tries to destroy you. You've tried everything, now try God. For the rest of your life see what He does. The Blessing is eternal life, not eternal death. You and your children need God in your life. Life is short, everyday is telling you this. A storm is coming in you're life one day as well as mine and everybody else. Nowadays the world is so crazy that no one is completely safe. Not in your home, car, school, or even walking down the street. Rich or poor, no exceptions. There are drugs and guns coming out of nowhere and people who are down think that there's no way out except to harm someone and take their money and possessions. This is from the heart. There is no other way to say it but to be truthful.

Pull yourself together people. Find a loving Church. One that preaches Christ. Above all things find that Christian Love. Those who come to church will find Christians who are not there to get in your business. They are there to help in any way they can. My dream is that our Christian brothers and sisters will always remember it's all about Jesus our Lord and Savior who bought all people with a price. It's not about you and me only. No profit from exploiting God's people. Remember that we are called to be chosen people to do His good works. Let's not lose those He called to serve Him. We can and will be accountable to God for everything we do. What would God do for a church that tries to do all the things He wants us to do?

I hope you know that every word or meaning came from the heart.

SALLIE'S WISE SUGGESTIONS

1. This is a subject that we may face sometime in our lives. If you live on you will get old. Our elders face many financial problems and have very little means of earning money. When the time comes of their departure from this world, the family that's left behind may be overwhelmed with bills and short on finances for burial.

If there are children left in the family - here is an idea. One or two of you go and get extra insurance on that elderly person. This isn't cruel, it's love. Doing it will take all of the pressure off of you and your siblings to pay this bill that is sure to come. It's up to you. If possible discuss the issue with your loved one. God Bless You.

2. Physical Storms come and go all the time. If your home is in harms way of the storm, MOVE. Get a U-Haul truck and place everything you don't want to lose in it. Do this as soon as you can before the storm comes and have it ready to move when it's time to evacuate. A day or two before, pack your car. Get a back pack and remember to include important papers, clean clothes, shoes and medications. Pack canned food if possible too.

Drive the U-Haul to a parking lot or safe place out of town. When the storm is over you can move back home if you're blessed to still have it. If you don't, at least you have your life and a new start.

UNTITLED ~ ODE TO A CHILD

    I stood, watched and listened as loved ones said their last goodbye. The parents, broken-hearted, hardly able to speak through their tears knowing that their child is gone and perhaps never to be seen by them again.

    I wondered did the child have any preparing in place? After all they were young and healthy. They may have only been thinking about what they would be doing tomorrow or who they would be meeting or who it was that they would fall in love with, all the while believing that there would be time for making it right with their Creator. They may have gone to Sunday School. They may have heard the preacher preach, but somewhere thought that death was for the old and after all "I am still very young", but without warning their opportunity was no more.

CONTRIBUTORS:

Joyce Walls
Melissa Greene
JAF
Jeffrey G. Mitchell Sr.
Keyshawna Johnson
Lynell Billingsley-Downer
Dr. Beverly Y. Murdock
Delois Langford
Evang. Adrianne Smiling
Sandra H. Murphy
Joyce Wilkerson
Dr. Alice Kelly
Vernae Taylor
Ernestine Jones
Ed Jones
Sallie Proctor
Tobias Pinckney
Willia Mae Edwards
Cindy Williams-Newsome (author Hobbstown)
Claudette Washington
Madeline Evans
Rocky Evans
Daryl Clark
Rev. Christian Nwakaihe
J. Handcock Williams
Rev. Dr. Doris J. Gray
Rev. Kyshon S. Mitchell
Rev. Lester Martin
Gail Downing
Evang. Tracy Fooster

To order additional copies of

POTPOURRI FROM THE HEART...

have your credit card ready and call
From USA: (800) 917-BOOK (2665)
From Canada: (877) 855-6732

or e-mail
orders@selahbooks.com

or order online at
www.selahbooks.com

2015
Blessings
Sister Gail
Darryl Clark (PG 94)
Sallie Proctor
Mother Mae